# WELLNESS THROUGH WORDS

*a multivocal anthology on healthcare, patient safety, and wellness*

# Praise

**Medical Gaslighting by Dr. Audrey Tang**

"Strongly recommended! The Gaslight Effect is real and very relevant, as the impact it can have on an individual, especially in our youth, is immeasurable. Dr Audrey's chapter provides an in-depth understanding of gaslighting and strategies to regain control of your own life. A must-read for authorities, educators, parents, and life/wellbeing coaches."

Ena Loum, British Novelist and Youth Advocate

**The Power of Connections by Sheila Brune**

"There could not possibly be a more appropriately named title for a chapter written by Sheila. Connections for Sheila are embedded in every aspect of her life: family, nursing, friends, community, and church, where she modeled how to make and grow connections to build fuller, happier lives."

Vicki Felger, RN, BA, MHCA, CPHQ (retired)

**Laughter is the Best Medicine ... For Nurses by Mary Frances Fisher**

"The author has a unique way of placing the reader at the scene as a spectator. She paints a very realistic portrait of what can and often does happen in a day's work as a bedside nurse."

Suzi Gard, RN

**How Childhood Trauma Surfaces and What To Do About It by Leslie Ferguson**

"Leslie Ferguson offers readers a profound gift in her chapter titled "How Childhood Trauma Surfaces and What We Can Do About It." A survivor of severe child abuse, including attempted murder by her own mother, Ms. Ferguson offers readers actionable tools for resilience. Grounded in research and personal experience, her ideas inspire hope. She clearly explains how early childhood trauma impacts health outcomes in survivors and provides evidence-based strategies to help survivors heal mentally, emotionally, and physically. She speaks with the authority of someone who has lived both the horror and the healing and has come out on top with wisdom to share."

Dr. Gina Simmons Schneider, PhD., licensed psychotherapist and author of *Frazzlebrain*

**Medical Encounters for Youth with Autism Spectrum Disorder by Lisa Jacovsky**

"In the article, *Medical Encounters for Youth with Autism Spectrum Disorder*, Ms. Jacovsky provides suggestions to assist healthcare providers with navigating different challenges that may arise when working with children with ASD. She offers various interventions that the health care providers can utilize in preparation for their patient's visit. Ms. Jacovsky's insights are simple, helpful, and extremely informative. As an educator, I find this article extremely helpful, not just for the healthcare field but in all scenarios."

Therese F. Sanders, M. Ed.

**Loss: One Common Thread by Donna Kincheloe**

"Donna carefully reveals and expounds on each step of the Kubler-Ross grieving process encountered by individuals who have experienced loss and educates those who care about them. By so doing, she has paved the way for healing those who are living with loss and grief, as well as empathy for those who strive to help them."

Adele M. Gill, retired RN and Chaplain

**Patient Fatigue by Rebecca Dimyan**

"Rebecca Dimyan puts readers into the shoes of a chronic illness patient, using concise prose rich with vivid imagery and sensory detail to invoke the emotions, fatigue, and frustration that come from dealing with an inadequate healthcare system on top of the symptoms of illness themselves. Everybody needs to read and take action on Dimyan's call to enact radical change to the way providers handle patients' needs and concerns."

Margaret Anne Mary Moore, author *Bold, Brave, and Breathless: Reveling in Childhood's Splendiferous Glories While Facing Disability and Loss*

**Living Well with Boundaries by Glen Alex**

"Have you ever asked yourself, 'Why does he keep doing that to me?' The answer is because they can." Glen guides readers through some complex psychological concepts, relationship dynamics, and internal processes in a succinct, accessible, and no-nonsense way. Glen also shares relatable examples so readers can walk away with a better understanding of themselves and their boundary journey ahead immediately."

Mynesha Whyte, MA, LPC - DEI practitioner, dance/movement psychotherapist, co-founder and President of Black Magic Association, Oakland, CA

**A Journey: Tick-Borne Illnesses and Mast Cell Activation Syndrome by Summer Le'Dawn**

"Summer provides an essential roadmap to help anyone suffering from a complex illness and not getting the help that they need. The combination of her personal experience and her extensive research into the complexities of treating mast cell activation syndrome and its causes is a very powerful story for all of us. No matter how sick or discouraged you feel, this will give you true hope and a way forward to feeling better."

Dr. Denise Clark, ND

**Healthy Adoptive Families Start with Self-Reflection by Tom Tracy**

"Adoption is beautiful and complex. Tom shares that sentiment throughout his writing. If you are considering adoption, this is a great place to start your research. Tom breaks down the types of adoption and the considerations with each one, especially transracial adoption. This information will only help adoptive parents be more prepared and better parents to adoptees."

Isaac Etter, Adoptee and Founder of Identity

**Your Health, Your Voice by Maria Papalia-Meier**

"I had the pleasure of meeting Maria during the early stages of her recovery. Having worked in the healthcare field for over 37 years, she stands out as an inspiration to me and so many others. Her willingness to step into and share her healing journey with such honesty continues to positively impact those affected by sepsis. For this, I am grateful."

Linda Jaros, Breath and Wellness Coach ~ Sports Muscular Therapist and Educator

**Reduce Anxiety and Heal Faster with a Surgery Coach by Chris Duffy Wentzel**

"Chris's journey of healing physically, emotionally, and spiritually is fascinating. Her journey is so compelling that I could not stop reading ... Her honesty touched my heart. She tells her life story with an open heart and recounts her insights and lessons in life."

Peggy Huddleston, Harvard researcher, therapist, and author *Prepare for Surgery Heal Faster*

**Parenting a Parent: Entering Their Reality by Alfredo Botello**

"This hits very close to home for me as my mother passed away from Alzheimer's dementia, and as a professional, I have worked with aging individuals and long-term care for over three decades. Alfredo shares his story in an open and heartfelt way that will surely resonate with many other people and can assist them in recognizing their own realities."

Sue Stillman Linja, RDN, LD, Author, *The Alzheimer's Prevention Food Guide*

**Stop Bullying and Amplifying Positive Childhood Experiences by Tom Dahlborg**

"Tom's chapter is a raw and powerful account of one family's journey from pain to purpose. Tom Dahlborg shares the heartbreaking story of almost losing his son to bullying, exposing how it can come from those we trust most and reminding us of our duty to prevent this manmade suffering. Through his son's story, Tom offers hope, practical guidance, and a call to give every child what they deserve—love and compassion."

Pantea Vahidi, RN, Founder of the Compassion Clinic ~ Leader of Compassion Circles

**Compassion is the Path by Nora D'Ecclesis**

"Dr. Nora D'Ecclesis has written an extraordinary chapter with her talent as a distinguished researcher and compassionate heart. The chapter explains the etymology of a mean-spirited archaic term directed toward a special needs population unable to defend against the emotional trauma that term inflicts."

Dr. George P. Bonner, D.C.M., Hall of Fame Inducted Physician, Author of *The Mindful Preschooler*, and *Zen Master of the Great Wave Sangha*

**Speak Up and Stay Alive by Patricia J. Rullo**

"You have a real gift for presenting deadly serious health issues in an engaging and entertaining way."

Mark S. Davis, MD, Operating room safety consultant and author of *Irresponsible: What Surgeons Won't Tell You and How to Protect Yourself*

# Contents

# Acknowledgements

I extend my heartfelt gratitude to the remarkable authors who have contributed their voices to this anthology. Your insights illuminate the intricate tapestry of the health and wellness journey, encompassing the perspectives of patients, caregivers, and medical professionals. Each contribution adds depth and richness to our collective vision of a safer, more compassionate health-related environment.

Your willingness to contribute personal stories, expert knowledge, and thoughtful reflections serves as a compelling invitation to take action. Together, you have crafted a powerful dialogue that challenges and inspires others to seek understanding and empathy in their own experiences. Thank you for your commitment to championing a holistic approach to wellness. Your efforts will resonate far beyond these pages, encouraging a greater awareness of the importance of safety and compassion in and out of the healthcare system.

Alfredo Botello, Amber Tresca, Andrea L. Wehlann, Arlene McCain, Audrey Tang, Chris Duffy-Wentzel, Donna Kincheloe, Ernest Ellender, Glen Alex, Leslie Ferguson, Lisa Charles, Lisa Jacovsky, Maria Bohle, Maria Papalia Meier, Mary Frances Fisher, Melissa Crook, Nora D'Ecclesis, Rebecca Dimyan, Sheila Brune, Summer Le'Dawn, Sweta Srivastava Vikram, Tia Warrick, Tom Dahlborg, Tom Tracy

With gratitude,

Patricia J. Rullo

# Introduction

*Wellness Through Words* is a collective effort to highlight the vital narratives that shape our experiences within the healthcare environment—narratives that speak to the heart of what it means to be both a patient and a caregiver. This anthology brings together the thoughts, insights, and creative expressions of twenty-five diverse authors—from seasoned medical professionals and mental health specialists to passionate patients and caregivers—who have graciously contributed their unique voices to a singular vision: a safer, more compassionate, and holistic approach to healthcare and wellbeing. Compiling diverse voices for this book is not just a literary endeavor but a clarion call for awareness, understanding, and empathy—fundamental elements for creating healing spaces in our medical institutions and within our lives.

**The Essence of Patient Safety**

When we speak of patient safety, we linger delicately on the precipice of life and death. The statistics are a harsh reminder that preventable medical errors cause injuries to millions of patients worldwide. These sobering facts reinforce the critical need for continuous dialogues around patient safety. The power of words can illuminate the systemic flaws in our healthcare systems, creating a path for open conversations about improvement. Through the shared narratives of this book, we aspire to foster a greater understanding of the role each individual plays in safeguarding their health and the health of their loved ones.

## Embracing Wellness

The pursuit of well-being extends beyond treating illness; it encompasses the full spectrum of human experience—mental, emotional, spiritual, and physical health. Wellness goes beyond the absence of disease and involves a holistic sense of being. Throughout these pages, you will encounter reflections from authors who share their journeys of recovery, resilience, and personal transformation. These stories remind us of the inevitable human experiences of suffering and joy and encourage us to embrace wellness as a proactive endeavor. The authors embrace wellness in myriad ways, creating a dialogue that is as layered as it is engaging. Their contributions underscore the importance of understanding the influences shaping our health and well-being, urging us to consider our own narratives while expanding our perspectives.

## Bridging the Gap

In healthcare, a gap often exists between what practitioners intend to convey and how patients receive and interpret that information. Through their stories, these authors confront the complexities of healthcare communication. Whether through the lens of making sense of a diagnosis, navigating the intricacies of treatment options, or finding one's voice in the face of adversity, the writings in this collection remind us that the connection between caregivers and patients should be rooted in trust, respect, and shared understanding.

## A Call to Action

As you immerse yourself in the stories and expressions on these pages, we encourage you to reflect on your own experiences. Ask yourself: How can we assert our voices? How can practitioners nurture an environment where openness and safety thrive? How can we work to embolden our communities to seek wellness in all its forms? To find the answers, we must look beyond medical textbooks and consider the personal experiences of those who intimately understand healthcare's consequences.

## A Collective Vision

"Wellness Through Words" is a movement towards a more enlightened and aware dialogue in healthcare. Each page offers an opportunity to delve deeper into the intricacies of patient safety, wellness, safe healthcare, and well-being. Let the words within these pages inspire you to question, advocate, and actively take part in creating a safer, more compassionate healthcare and wellness experience—one word, one story at a time.

# Chapter 1

## Patient Fatigue

Rebecca Dimyan

Thin, scratchy white paper sticks to cold, bare legs. It is January, but it seems as if the doctor's office has air conditioning cranked up instead of the heat. Nothing about the room is comforting. The beige walls, devoid of pictures or artwork, are mostly empty except for medical infographics and diagrams of the human body. Bright fluorescent lights create an environment that feels more like a display than an examining room.

I am a patient, but I feel like a spectacle.

*Come one! Come all! Check out this malfunctioning body! Unhealthy organs like you've never seen before!*

*I am a freak in a sideshow, and this is Coney Island. The doctor is not a medical professional but a spectator in a parade of unending spectators who show up to marvel, question, poke, prod, laugh, dismiss, assert, maybe diagnose, but probably misdiagnose, and then move on to the next chronically ill curiosity.*

This is the circus that plays out in my head at every doctor appointment I've had in the past year. The reality is that I am a sick patient, waiting to see yet another new doctor, hoping for a diagnosis. It is 2016. I have been experiencing pelvic and abdominal pain for nearly eight years. I am thirty years old, and I am over it. Over all of it. I have patient fatigue. Burn out.

However, one positive outcome of this generally unpleasant experience is that I have mastered the art of the medical process. Schedule an appointment with a new doctor. Fill out the forms. Relay the symptoms in all the gritty details. Repeat. I should probably type everything up at this point and make copies that I can distribute, like the minutes of a meeting at each new office—*left side pelvic and abdominal pain. The pain scale is inefficient at best, but let's call it an eight because I'm able to walk, sort of. I'd describe it as cramping, sharp, piercing. Sometimes nausea. The pain wakes me up. The pain worsens after sex.*

At this stage in my medical journey, I've seen them all: gastroenterologist, endocrinologist, gynecologist, ER doctor, general practitioner. I even consulted Web MD, and, no surprise, it was quite certain that I was dying. Each specialist reads my pain narrative through their own lens: the gastro was certain I had IBS and was shocked when the colonoscopy and endoscopy came up clean. The general practitioner said it was thyroid, and the ER doctor said it was resolved because it was an ovarian cyst that had already ruptured. The third or fourth gynecologist finally diagnosed me with endometriosis, a chronic condition where tissue similar to the lining of the uterus grows on other organs. It can cause pain, infertility, and a host of other complications. After spending nearly a decade chasing this diagnosis, it is no wonder that I felt like a freak in a sideshow. My experience with pain and sickness was ignored, dismissed, invalidated, or misunderstood. So many doctors did not take me seriously. I was simply entertainment—or worse.

Although my chronic illness story is, unfortunately, not uncommon, it did have a happy ending. After a series of failed doctors' appointments, which only left me frustrated and no closer to improvement, I met with a gynecologist who made it her mission to get me answers. She performed a laparoscopy a month after our initial visit. During this minimally invasive surgical procedure, she located and eradicated endometriosis lesions on my ovary and bowel. Confident she had fixed my chronic pain problem, she was dismayed when the pelvic and abdominal suffering persisted post-surgery. The treatment had failed, but she had given me something almost as valuable: a diagnosis. Once I knew the reason behind my discomfort, I ultimately found a holistic path that led me to relief and management with Eastern medicine.

The healthcare system is broken, but light shines through the cracks. Kind nurses and determined doctors exist who genuinely want to help. They are not unicorns; they are real, and I am grateful for them. These were the people who listened and did everything they could to help me. When I think about how we can improve patient care and treatment, I think about these unsung heroes and the tools they lack.

Perhaps a more holistic approach to medicine is one such tool. Doctors are taught to treat symptoms and eliminate the pain, discomfort, and illness. But here's a crazy idea: what if they don't? What if they don't simply treat the problems as singular issues and, instead, consider the health of the whole body? The body as the complicated, messy, whole person that it is? What if they brought some holistic philosophies and care into Western medical practices? What if a patient was made to feel like an art exhibit instead of a sideshow? The medical industry can start with a simple first step: respecting our stories. We are human beings— we are not our illnesses. We are sick, but we are more than chronic conditions. And our experiences are worthy of appreciation.

With experience comes knowledge and, sometimes, wisdom. I have learned my body, my triggers, and every nuance of my chronic disease. I am also fluent in the language of patients. Now, I know how to speak and act to get treatment and results. I know that I must be my own advocate. Far too often, my voice has been soft and sweet. Sometimes, I need to speak loudly, or at least assertively, to ensure I am heard.

Here is what I've learned on my way to finding diagnosis and treatment:

1. **Tell your story your way.** The language of medicine is limiting. Sometimes, the words they offer us are inadequate in capturing

the tone, the tempo, the very essence of our pain, our conditions, and our symptoms. Find your own language. Invent words if you need to. Articulate every excruciating detail of your experience. It is your story. Own it. Share it. Make them listen.

2. **Do not give up.** This may seem trite, obvious, or cliché, but it is so important and surprisingly easy to forget. Do not let anyone dismiss or minimize your pain or discomfort. It is yours. You know it. You live it. Find a doctor who makes you feel seen.

3. **Do your research**. I am in no way encouraging you to consult Google or Web MD to diagnose or treat your illness; however, when you get answers, don't just assume that what your doctor says is gospel. Ask questions. Lots of questions. Read books and articles. Find discussion boards and support groups. Ask them questions. Become an expert in your illness. Keep an open mind. Western medicine is helpful, but Eastern medicine is too. Don't limit yourself to one proscribed path to healing.

4. **Seek community**. Illness is isolating. It is easy to disappear into a miasma of despair when unwell. Our loved ones often don't understand what we are going through on a physiological or mental level. You may feel that you are all alone and find yourself fading from your own life, subsumed by your illness. Go online. Social media hasn't always been known to bring people together; however, in this instance, it is a wonderful place to seek out others who are in similar situations. They may be strangers, but perhaps it is in connecting with these strangers that we will find some previously unknown part of ourselves. Perhaps we will find understanding, support, and maybe even peace.

5. **Give yourself grace.** You will become frustrated, tired, and likely experience many dark, negative emotions. Embrace those feelings. They are valid. Don't forget to show yourself kindness and love.

It can be difficult, but in the most challenging moments, remember to breathe. Although things may seem beyond your control, you are the ringmaster of this chronic illness circus. You decide what your next act will be.

**About the Author**

Rebecca Dimyan is an award-winning writer, editor, and teacher. Her work has been published in national and international publications, including *Vox, the CT Post, YahooHealth, 34th Parallel, Glassworks Magazine, The Mighty*, and many others. She has taught college writing at several Connecticut universities for over a decade. Rebecca is also an experienced editor and conference director. Her memoir *Chronic* was published in 2023 and delves into her experience with chronic illness and alternative medicine. Her debut novel *Waiting for Beirut* was a 2021 Fairfield Book Prize finalist. Both books won the 2023 Firebird Book Awards.

rebeccadimyanwriter.com

rdimyan@gmail.com

# Chapter 2

# Medical Gaslighting

Dr. Audrey Tang

**Let's talk about "medical gaslighting."**

"Gaslight", written in the late 1930s, told the story of one man's obsession with wealth, which led to him systematically manipulating his wife into thinking she was going mad. The behaviors identified throughout the play have given rise to the term "gaslighting" – a long-term, systematic manipulation of someone's thinking. This manipulation makes the individual unable to trust their judgment, making them completely dependent on the gaslighter. Unfortunately, this behavior can occur in professional contexts, such as in a medical setting. However, it's important to emphasize that in professional settings, the motives behind "gaslighting" are unlikely to be as manipulative or personal as when it happens in an intimate or family relationship.

In an under-resourced, overworked, and cost-conscious profession, healthcare providers may not always receive adequate training or support, and at times, they may be burned out. As a result, patients may be dismissed as having "nothing to worry about" even when they are clearly experiencing a health issue.

The practical or systemic reasons are plentiful:

- Perhaps it isn't showing on the tests they may have had (note, however, this can also be due to long wait times or delays.)

- The medical professional isn't trained
- Something may have been overlooked – perhaps due to short consultation times
- Mistakes *can* happen

**What Might Happen?**

**Example 1: A belief that the "Doctor knows all"**

I know people who have experienced this personally. In some cases, necessary action was only taken after a second opinion revealed issues such as thyroid problems, cancer, and endometriosis. It's worth noting that it can take up to 7 years for endometriosis to be correctly diagnosed, with the person affected having to continually push for help.

If the patient believes the doctor is the ultimate authority due to factors such as age, culture, or context, they may be hesitant to seek a second opinion or may ask so timidly that the doctor dismisses them. The doctor, believing they are right or lacking the resources, time, or energy to change their opinion, may also reject the idea of a second opinion and may dismiss them again.

**Example 2: False assumptions**

Another example that could fall within inappropriate communication between doctor and patient comes from the research of Professor Sharon Hinchliff, who works on the sexual rights of older adults. In her interviews, she has found that general practitioners sometimes deliberately do not explain the sexual side effects to an "older" patient. In contrast, they would to a younger one, believing that "sex is a private matter for older patients." This is very biased and potentially detrimental and throws "informed consent" into question. Sex may well be a private matter, but side effects are indeed a general one.

**Example 3: Fear of reprisal**

Sometimes, "gaslighting" can be done to protect oneself from potential legal action. For example, my late father, who was blind, experienced an incident during his dialysis where someone accidentally poked his vein. As a result, the dialysis procedure that day was unsuccessful, and he experienced swelling. However, when he was picked up, the staff quickly blamed him, saying, "he moved his arm." I have to believe my father on this (who says he didn't move), but he didn't want me to complain for fear of possible mistreatment because he was blind and, therefore, more vulnerable.

I quickly did my own research and realized that, unfortunately, these things DO happen. I explained to my father that if it were to happen again with the same person, then we would have to say something as it might be easily fixed with further training. However, the senior team cared for him the next time he attended, and everything went well.

But again, while not malicious in intent, mistakes can happen, and blaming the patient can be a way to avoid any repercussions.

**"Watch and Wait" is a Real Thing.**

Dismissing benign symptoms might be considered a diagnosis of something being benign and could also involve the reasonable approach of "watch and wait." Why subject someone to an invasive treatment unnecessarily? However, given the overwhelmed state of some healthcare services, one might wonder if "watch and wait" is being used because the service is too oversubscribed to take any action.

The motivation for watching and waiting is key. If the patient shows evidence of a problem that is dismissed, for example, because it came from a "work health check" rather than the GP surgery, I would urge you to ask if the surgeon can re-run the test.

I have a personal example to share. I brought my own blood test results to my doctor, which showed an iron deficiency. Initially, my doctor said, "We can't accept these results." I responded, "But you can order a blood test," and he did. I was then prescribed ferrous fumarate.

Another issue can arise if certain symptoms mask others, and the symptoms that are overlooked are not the serious ones. The person may have omitted mentioning other symptoms because they themselves deemed them unimportant.

We must remember that GPs are "general" practitioners and are only as good as their training. For instance, if a doctor is not trained in discussing menopause, they may misdiagnose symptoms of menopause or perimenopause as depression and anxiety caused by stress. However, asking more questions could reveal that the symptoms are actually related to menopause or perimenopause.

Diagnosis should be a two-way process. Our voices matter as we live within our bodies 24/7.

**Practical Tools to Address Medical Gaslighting.**

While it is natural to be concerned about raising an issue or potentially causing conflict, remember that this is simply a discussion. A lot of emotional worry and anxiety can be removed if you stick to discussing facts and evidence. As such, record-keeping becomes essential.

**Pre-consultation**

- Keep a record (including photos if applicable) of your symptoms so you can show them to the doctor. You may feel rushed or be drawn off track during an appointment, but by writing things down, especially when they happen, you have the evidence to shape and guide your conversation. Leave a copy with the doctor if you wish. If you have test results from previous visits, include those in the evidence. This can also prevent dismissal over "the same thing." You can say that it has already been "tested for," for example

- Ask someone you trust—and perhaps who can appraise and process the situation cognitively and unemotionally—to attend your consultation to take notes and remind you of the agenda you wish to discuss. (If you feel emotional during the consultation, you will have someone focused on your needs.)

~ Explain your concerns to them

~ Outline what you hope to achieve from the consultations

~ Be clear about what you'd like them to do. For example, please make sure that all the following questions are asked. If you notice something amiss, can you jump in and ask if I forgot?

- You might want to research your consultant before meeting them. If they are not a specialist in the field, you can mention this during the consultation.

**Within the consultation**

If you bring someone in with you, you may need to clear it with reception. However, this is not usually an issue outside the extra restrictions due to the pandemic.

- In consultation, if you are being told something you are unsure about, ask, "Can you explain that in more detail?"

Other questions include:

- What research is that based on?
- How do you interpret test results?
- What have you recommended to other patients in my position?

- What other options are there?
- Is there someone I could see who is a specialist in this area?

When you are unsure why you may be dismissed, ask, "Why do you think that?" Also, inquire about your next steps and the expected timeline for treatment by asking, "What are my next steps?" and "What is my expected timeline for treatment?" Furthermore, you have the legal right to request a copy of your test results and medical records.

**Following the consultation**

- Keep a record of the meeting and the next steps.
- If you are worried, seek a second opinion—you do not necessarily need to pay for a private one.
- Before you leave, ask your practice to refer you to another doctor.
- If it's a consultant, ask your GP if they will refer you to a different consultant.

Following your second opinion, make an appointment with the first consultant/doctor to discuss the second opinion and treatment options. (It's okay to seek a third opinion, although you may need to pay for that one.) Then, return to discuss the results if they differ.

- Continue to document your symptoms
- If you are still concerned about how you have been treated, please contact your Trust's PALS liaison, The Patient Advice and Liaison Service (in the UK). Similar patient advocacy services exist across the US healthcare system. Provide them with your evidence and outline your whole situation. End with a "call to action," stating your expectation of a written response within ten working days addressing specific points.

- Be aware that legal action is always an option. This process, which involves your record keeping, also compiles a bundle of evidence in case it's needed for court.

While the medical profession has a wealth of knowledge and experience, it's important to remember that we know our bodies best. Please speak up if you feel you aren't getting the answers you need. Even if you decide against a second opinion or a different test, your comments and concerns will still have to be noted at that moment.

My very best to you.

## About the Author

Dr. Audrey Tang is a chartered psychologist (British Psychological Society) and award-winning business author focused on practical tools for well-being. She founded Wellbeing Media Studio, broadcasting her shows "Mental Health Matters" and "Skits and Quibbles" (the arts and wellbeing show globally from Feb 2024) while providing a media platform to the local community. She created the podcast 'Retrain Your Brain for Success' (winner of the Positive Change podcast awards in both the Mental Health and Self Improvement categories); and The Wellbeing Lounge on NLive Radio (winning 2nd place Female Presenter of the Year 2022 & 2023, with the show shortlisted as "Specialist Content Show of the Year", Community Radio Awards), and provided psychology contribution to Channel 4's "Don't Diet Lose Weight", and The Chrissy B Show (Sky).

She continues to offer expert comments as a psychologist spokesperson both academically and through TV, radio, and published media in the fields of mindfulness, resilience, leadership, and wellbeing. Audrey is a qualified teacher (QTS), CPD accredited trainer, Leadership Development coach (ICF), and FIRO-B (relationship) profiler working within organizations. As well as her mental and emotional fitness workshops (webinar/in person) and coaching practice, she is a long-time advocate for boosting confidence through her community work with CLICK Productions (a theatre group she founded in 1993), offering opportunities to build confidence, boost self-value and learn new skills through shows and performing arts events which she has now turned into the Charity CLICK Arts Foundation, and teaches Burlesque for body confidence alongside running wellbeing events.

draudreyt.com

hello@draudreyt.com

# Chapter 3

# Your Health, Your Voice

Maria Papalia Meier

When it comes to your healthcare, do you feel like you have control, or do you put your health in the hands of your medical care team? Do you feel you have the right to get a second opinion? My husband and I learned a lot through my healthcare journey. I have been fortunate to speak with people from all over the world and share what I have learned from our experience, empowering them to take control of their health when talking to their healthcare providers.

I will start by sharing some lessons learned from my journey and then some advice demonstrating the importance of advocating for yourself.

**My Sepsis Story**

When telling my sepsis story, I make it a point to say I went into septic shock from a strep infection I didn't know I had. I thought I had the flu. When I wasn't feeling well, I called my doctor's office and provided them with SOME of my symptoms: I was achy, had chills, and felt weak. The nurse concluded from our call that these symptoms pointed to the flu. She advised me to rest and call in a few days if I wasn't feeling better.

Had I mentioned that I had a rash on my stomach that eventually spread to my arms and that I thought I was dehydrated because my urine was a light Coca-Cola color, the conversation I had with the nurse may have gone differently. It might have prompted them to ask more questions or have me come into the office earlier. The outcome could have been different if I had given more information.

You see, doctors and nurses are not mind readers. They can only provide a diagnosis from the symptoms you give them, so you must provide them with any new symptoms or markings you may have noticed.

**Know Where to Go**

Are you familiar with the hospitals in your area? If you needed to go to the hospital, would you know which would provide the best care? When my husband and I moved to Massachusetts from Georgia, we didn't realize the importance of knowing the surrounding hospitals in case of an emergency. We learned a lesson we will never forget.

When we went to the doctor's office on June 18th, we had no idea how sick I was. I arrived at the exam room, and an ambulance was called shortly after. The doctor asked which hospital we preferred. We selected a nearby hospital, thinking it was a good choice, but it turned out to be a relatively small one that wasn't fully equipped to handle the severity of my illness.

**Time to Amputate! Wait, What?**

Because of the medication I was given to maintain organ function, my blood flow to my extremities was restricted, which resulted in my feet turning black from my ankles to the tips of my toes.

During my hospital stay, I consulted with a skilled vascular surgeon, and after being discharged, I had multiple follow-up appointments with him. The vascular doctor was proficient in his field, and I felt privileged to be under his care. My feet were doing what is called "self-amputating." Dead skin would fall off, and new skin would grow. I knew all along that losing my toes was most likely going to happen, and honestly, after what I had gone through, it was a small price to pay. But I was not prepared for what the doctor told me on one of our visits. He told my husband and me he felt my feet were done "healing," and it was time to amputate. He suggested doing a trans metatarsal amputation, which would have taken most of the front part of my feet. This was a huge decision I was uncomfortable making at the time. It was not an emergency where my life was in danger, so we told him we would like to seek a second opinion from an orthopedic doctor. We were referred to a foot and ankle specialist who looked at my feet and referred me to the Wound Center in Boston.

The second opinion opened a new path for me. This alternative approach facilitated the healing of my feet and enabled me to preserve more of my feet, ultimately expediting my recovery process.

I felt anxious and scared when I went for a second opinion and met with the orthopedist. The condition of my toes made me worried they could fall off, particularly my pinky toes. I was extremely apprehensive and would overreact whenever the orthopedist touched my feet. He was understanding but said, if you want to keep more of your foot, you must find a way to make it through your appointments. He suggested speaking to someone and getting on some meds if necessary but emphasized the importance of finding a solution. When I left his office that day, I was taken aback. No one had been that direct with me before, but I needed it, and I am forever grateful for that conversation. I often hear it when I am too "afraid" to do something.

My new path brought me to the Wound Center in Boston. I went once a week to have my feet debrided, and in time, the doctor said it was time to amputate. I had all my toes amputated, but I was able to keep most of my foot. Learning to walk and eventually run was made easier.

**A Few Takeaways**

- I was seeing a top doctor, yet his advice and recommendations were based on his knowledge and expertise in his field. This doesn't make it wrong; it just doesn't make it the only answer.

- Second opinions are important before doing anything major. My recovery and outcome improved because I could keep more of my foot.

- Communication is key. Your doctors can only help you if they know everything that is going on.

- Know which hospitals are best for what. If you are admitted and find that your hospital cannot treat you, ask for a transfer.

**Other Examples**

I noticed a small pimple-like sore on my left foot with a white head. Upon examination, I was told that it was likely a blister and given instructions on how to care for it properly. Time went by, and the site was still sore, and I was experiencing a low-grade fever. After all I had been through, I scheduled a follow-up appointment with my primary doctor. She tested the fluid in the sore, which was positive for MRSA. Upon being prescribed antibiotics, I promptly arranged a follow-up consultation with my podiatrist. The MRI scan revealed the presence of a bone infection, leading to a surgical procedure that involved the removal of five bones.

MRSA can get into your bloodstream and cause death if not treated right away. Knowing what can cause MRSA and the signs is vital.

I recently went to see my oncologist because I have the BRCA gene for breast and ovarian cancer. At my last checkup, I talked about my weight gain and how it was having a negative effect on me. I went into my appointment knowing I wanted to talk about checking my hormone levels. I mentioned to her that I was thinking of seeing a woman who was a board-certified functional health practitioner certified in hormone health. She told me she would not advise me to do any hormone replacement, take any prescriptions, or do anything over the counter.

We had an open conversation about it, and in the end, she told me she couldn't tell me what to do. She assured me she would always be there to advise. However, because I have the BRCA gene, taking anything containing estrogen by mouth puts me at risk. She also said the medicine I had been on for the last five years to reduce my risk of breast cancer is an estrogen suppressor. The dialogue was highly valuable as she gave me insight into her perspective on the flaws of my plan. I know she only had my best interest in mind. Even though I didn't like what she had to say, she gave me a reason to pause and rethink.

I've been under the care of a foot and ankle specialist. Over the years, I've always felt comfortable contacting him with any issues. When I experienced a recent knee issue, he recommended a specialist who could assist. He also suggested that I see a doctor specializing in treating runners. He mentioned that this doctor takes a comprehensive approach, considering my medical history and providing care for my entire body.

It was this doctor who suggested an MRI of my knee. Thanks to the MRI, the necrosis was caught early, potentially preventing the need for surgery. He also recommended that I give shockwave therapy a try, and I've just finished my treatments.

## Communication, Communication, Communication

In my examples, you can see how communication is key. Don't let your healthcare professionals guess the issue. Tell them all the symptoms you may be having.

Once you receive a diagnosis, do research. One of the best ways is to find others who have been through the same thing. There are plenty of us out there. People with serious illnesses or accidents want to help others by sharing their stories. While your journey may differ, this will help you start a dialogue with your healthcare team.

Unless medically necessary, don't rush into anything that can drastically change your quality of life without getting a second opinion. That second opinion can change your path.

Too often, I hear people feel dismissed or brushed off by their healthcare professionals. They know something is wrong but are being informed otherwise. Trust your instincts and seek answers until you are satisfied with the care and information you receive. Be your own advocate and make sure your voice is heard throughout your healthcare journey.

**About the Author**

On June 18, 2014, my life was changed forever. I had just turned 40. As a mom of two young children and a wife, I had it all: a great career and a loving family. Life was good. Things changed 15 days after my 40th birthday. I was in the hospital fighting for my life; I had gone into septic shock. I spent a little over seven weeks between the hospital and rehab and came home on August 8th.

"Celebrate the little victories in life; those can lead to the biggest changes." This phrase came to me during my run. I had to be reminded by my husband of the things I was doing and how far I had come and not of what I could no longer do, which for me was running. My outlook and perspective only changed when I started looking at the positives and stopped focusing on the negatives. I was mad for a while, wondering why me. Losing my toes was a bigger hurdle than I thought it was going to be, and as a runner, being told I would never run again was pure devastation. I started the #toelessrunner to take something that happened to me and turn it into something positive and show others that no matter what, you can reach any goals you set your mind to. My road was not easy, and it wasn't short either; it took many years of hard work and a series of ups and downs to get where I am today, but I made it. I have run numerous 1/2 marathons and the Kiawah Island Marathon on December 10, 2022.

Life doesn't always go as planned, but sometimes God's plan is far better. I can honestly say I am living my best life!

thetoelessrunner.com

pap3919@gmail.com

# CHAPTER 4

# THE SYMPHONY OF HAPPINESS: A DANCE OF THE BRAIN AND BODY

LISA CHARLES

Happiness isn't some mystical force that descends upon us—it's a complex dance between the brain and body. Working as the Fitness/Wellness Research Coordinator at Rutgers University's Aging & Brain Health Alliance gave me a fascinating window into this intricate choreography. There, I witnessed firsthand the profound impact of how sleep, nourishment, and movement create a melody of well-being. Each factor plays a vital restorative force in the symphony of happiness. Every choice we make, thoughts, and actions we take add another note to this symphony, shaping the quality of our lives and our overall sense of fulfillment. When the brain and body are aligned, we position ourselves to experience a more joyful existence.

**Neurotransmitters: The Maestros of Mood**

Imagine the brain as a grand concert hall, where neurotransmitters—our chemical messengers—take the stage as the maestros of mood. Dopamine, the "reward chemical," surges with each triumph, igniting motivation for new pursuits. It's the exhilarating feeling of crossing the finish line, achieving a long-held goal, or simply savoring a delicious meal. This neurotransmitter drives us to seek more positive experiences, fueling the cycle of happiness.

Serotonin, the "feel-good chemical," bathes us in contentment, regulating sleep and weaving a tapestry of well-being. It's the calm satisfaction we experience after a good night's rest, a warm embrace, or a moment of quiet reflection. Serotonin is crucial in maintaining a balanced mood and inner peace.

Endorphins, nature's painkillers, take the spotlight during physical activity, dulling discomfort and elevating mood. It's the runner's high, the post-workout glow, and the feeling of accomplishment that comes from pushing our physical limits. These natural opioids create a crescendo of positive feedback, motivating us to continue moving and strengthening our bodies.

Exercise becomes a maestro's baton, summoning a chorus of endorphins and dopamine. Even a brisk walk can rewrite the negative moments of our day, enhancing mood and nurturing brain cells with neurotrophic factors, their fertilizer for growth and resilience. These factors promote the birth of new neurons and strengthen existing connections, creating a more robust and adaptable brain prepared to meet life's daily challenges.

**The Gut-Brain Axis: A Symphony of Microbes**

In recent years, science has unveiled a surprising twist in the symphony of happiness: the gut-brain axis. The trillions of bacteria residing in our gut, the microbiome, play an unexpected role in this orchestration. They influence the production of neurotransmitters, particularly serotonin, suggesting a profound gut-brain connection.

Emerging research indicates that an imbalance in gut bacteria, known as dysbiosis, may contribute to mood disorders such as depression and anxiety. This is because the gut microbiome influences the production of neurotransmitters, particularly serotonin, which plays a crucial role in regulating mood. This discovery opens exciting possibilities for future treatments. Could manipulating this microbiome through diet or probiotics be a future movement in the composition of happiness?

Nourishing our gut becomes akin to tending a flourishing garden, where diverse and beneficial bacteria thrive. A balanced diet rich in probiotics and fiber nurtures this internal ecosystem, potentially increasing serotonin production and fostering a positive outlook. Fermented foods like yogurt, sauerkraut, and kimchi, along with fiber-rich fruits, vegetables, and whole grains, provide the nourishment these beneficial microbes need to flourish.

Incorporating prebiotic foods and fueling probiotics can further enhance the gut microbiome's symphony. Foods like garlic, onions, asparagus, and bananas contain prebiotics that promote the growth of beneficial bacteria. By tending to our gut health, we support digestion and immunity and cultivate a more harmonious relationship between our gut and brain, influencing our mood and overall well-being. Prebiotics and probiotics promote the growth of beneficial bacteria and help maintain a healthy balance of gut flora, which is essential for serotonin production and a positive outlook.

## Mindfulness: Tuning the Instrument of the Mind

Our brains are not passive instruments, but orchestras we can tune through mindfulness. Daily breathing exercises, body scans, or mindful walking can become our practice, focusing on the present moment, the ebb and flow of breath, sensations, and thoughts. This practice calms the mind, reducing stress hormones like cortisol. Chronic stress can dampen the symphony of happiness, as cortisol can impair cognitive function, disrupt sleep, and contribute to various health problems.

By strengthening the prefrontal cortex, the conductor of decision-making and emotional regulation, mindfulness allows us to mute negativity and amplify positivity. We can breathe in joy while releasing stressful thoughts. It empowers us to respond to life's challenges with greater resilience. Research suggests that mindfulness can increase gray matter in the brain, particularly in areas associated with learning, memory, and emotional regulation. Mindfulness interventions can also be effective as effective as medication in treating anxiety and depression.

**Sleep: The Master Composer of Harmony**

Just as a conductor shapes a performance, sleep orchestrates the body's symphony of health. During sleep's restorative embrace, tissues mend, memories solidify, and hormones find balance. It's a time of deep rejuvenation, essential for physical and mental well-being.

Sleep deprivation, like a dissonant note, disrupts this harmony, leading to cognitive fog, emotional instability, and a weakened immune system. When we don't sleep enough, our brains struggle to consolidate memories, make decisions, and regulate emotions. We become more irritable, anxious, stressed, and prone to errors.

Sleep deprivation can wreak havoc on the body's symphony of health, causing issues across various systems:

- Brain Fog and Reduced Cognitive Function: Imagine the strings of a violin losing their tension, creating discordant notes. Sleep deprivation disrupts communication between brain cells, leading to difficulty concentrating, remembering information, and making decisions.

- Irritability and Emotional Dysregulation: Think of a flute player struggling to control their breath, leading to erratic and unpleasant notes. Lack of sleep can impair emotional regulation, making us more prone to outbursts of anger, anxiety, and sadness.

- Weakened Immune System: Imagine the backstage crew neglecting their duties, allowing germs to infiltrate the performance. Sleep deprivation weakens the immune system, making us more susceptible to illness and hindering recovery from existing ones. One cannot overestimate the importance of a robust immune system with COVID-related struggles fresh in our minds.

Like an orchestra that hasn't had enough rehearsal, a sleep-deprived body struggles to perform at its best. Cognitive function declines, reaction times slow, and mood can become unstable. However, prioritizing sleep allows the body to rehearse its vital functions, ensuring a harmonious performance in the symphony of health. Restorative sleep can ignite a pathway to joy and inner peace.

In the symphony of health, sleep acts as the master conductor, ensuring each instrument performs in perfect harmony. Just as a well-rested orchestra delivers a flawless performance, sufficient sleep allows the body's systems to work together seamlessly. During sleep, the body enters a vital state, repairing tissues, consolidating memories, and regulating hormones – all crucial for optimal physical and mental function.

**Movement: The Pulse of the Symphony**

Regular physical activity is essential for conducting your symphony of health and happiness. There are many ways to get moving, each with unique benefits:

**Cardiovascular Exercise**: This is your heart's best friend. Cardio gets your blood pumping, strengthens your heart and lungs, and improves overall fitness. Think of it as the rhythm section of your symphony, setting the beat for a healthier you. Examples include:

- Brisk walking, running, or jogging
- Swimming
- Biking (indoors or outdoors)
- Dancing (aerobics, Zumba, or just for fun!)

- Elliptical training

**Strength Training**: These exercises build muscle mass and strength, like adding powerful brass instruments to your orchestra. Strength training helps maintain bone density, boost metabolism, and improve posture. Examples include:

- Lifting weights (free weights, machines, or kettlebells)
- Bodyweight exercises (push-ups, squats, lunges)
- Resistance bands

**Flexibility Exercises**: Think of these as the graceful movements of a ballet dancer, improving your range of motion and keeping joints healthy. They can also reduce muscle tension and improve posture. Examples include:

- Yoga
- Pilates
- Tai Chi
- Stretching routines

**Low-Impact Exercises**: These gentler options are perfect for beginners or those with joint issues. They offer many benefits without putting excessive stress on your body. Imagine a soothing melody played on a harp. Examples include:

- Walking
- Water aerobics
- Gentle Yoga or Pilates

### Finding Your Rhythm in Movement

The best exercise for you is the one you enjoy and can stick with. It's about finding your unique rhythm in the symphony of movement. Consider your preferences, fitness level, and any health concerns. Remember, even small amounts of physical activity (10 minutes) can make a big difference. Start slowly, gradually increase the intensity and duration, and most importantly, have fun!

### The Conductor's Baton: Crafting a Symphony of Well-Being

Understanding this intricate dance empowers us to conduct our symphony of happiness:

**Move with intention**: Physical activity, from a brisk walk to vigorous exercise, awakens endorphins and cultivates resilience. It strengthens our hearts, lungs, and muscles, providing a foundation for long-term health and happiness. Aim for at least 150 minutes of moderate-intensity exercise or 75 minutes of vigorous-intensity exercise each week, spread throughout the week.

**Nourish the gut**: A balanced diet rich in probiotics and fiber nurtures the microbiome's positive influence on mood. Incorporate fermented foods like yogurt, sauerkraut, and kimchi, as well as fiber-rich fruits, vegetables, and whole grains.

**Embrace mindfulness**: Daily meditation and mindful breathing tune the instrument of the mind, enhancing emotional awareness. Even a few minutes of quiet reflection each day can make a difference.

**Prioritize sleep:** Like a well-rested orchestra, a well-rested body performs optimally. Aim for 7-8 hours of quality sleep each night. Create a relaxing bedtime routine, avoid caffeine and alcohol before bed, and ensure your sleep environment is cool, dark, and quiet.

**Cultivate connections**: Nurturing solid relationships creates a harmonious social environment. Spend time with loved ones, engage in meaningful conversations, and offer support and encouragement. Social connection is a fundamental human need and is crucial to our happiness.

**Pursue passions**: Engaging in joyful activities adds vibrancy and meaning to life's melody. Whether painting, playing music, gardening, or volunteering, make time for the things that ignite your soul.

### A Symphony in Progress

The science of happiness is a thrilling exploration that unfolds like a constantly revised map. Every discovery about the brain-body connection reveals another hidden pathway to well-being. Future research may unveil the influence of our environment on the gut microbiome or the intricate dance between social connection and neurotransmitter production. We may even discover the precise biological mechanisms behind the power of mindfulness.

Despite the ongoing quest for knowledge, the core message remains a powerful truth: I hold the power to influence my happiness. By incorporating these evidence-based strategies, I become the conductor of my well-being orchestra, harmonizing the instruments of my body and mind. This symphony of happiness isn't a static performance; it's a continuous composition, evolving with every choice I make. Every brisk walk, nutritious meal, mindful breath, and moment of connection with loved ones adds another note to the melody of joy. The beauty lies in knowing that I am not a passive audience member in the theater of happiness; I am the active composer, wielding the baton of intention and self-care to create a life that resonates with fulfillment.

## About the Author

Lisa is an award-winning keynote speaker and the best-selling author of *Yes! Commit. Do. Live*, a book centered on training people to tap into the brain-body connection, enabling them to embrace any passion and desire and turn it into tangible results. Lisa is also the CEO of Embrace Your Fitness, LLC, a wellness consultancy driven to bring innovative, creative, and effective Wellness programs to individuals, corporations, and organizations.

After serving as a federal prosecutor and singer/actress, Lisa found a passion for wellness as a coach and trainer after successfully shedding 77 pounds without dieting using her signature "Commit. Do. Live" strategy. She then served as the Fitness/Wellness Research Coordinator for the Rutgers University Aging & Brain Health Alliance.

Now, as a Brain, Body, and Belief Alignment Expert, Lisa specializes in sleep management and breathing techniques. She empowers corporate employees and individuals to let go of their limiting beliefs, find their creativity, embrace who they are, and break through any age-limiting barriers by allowing them to experience wellness from her top-down, inside-out approach.

She is the co-creator of Reinventing the Women Mastery group and the provider of international retreats that help individuals experience the Age-Defying Life by releasing stress, renewing energy, and restoring sleep while gaining the mental clarity to live the life of their dreams.

YesCoachLisa.com

lisa@YesCoachLisa.com

# Chapter 5

## Stop Bullying and Amplifying Positive Childhood Experiences

Tom Dahlborg

"Mom. Dad. I need to tell you something. When I was in fourth grade, the pain was so great, I put a belt around my neck—I didn't want to live anymore."

Victims of bullying are between 2 to 9 times more likely to consider suicide than non-victims, according to studies by Yale University.

That discussion with our son occurred a year after I published the first edition of our stop-bullying book, *The Big Kid and Basketball ... and the Lessons he taught his Father and Coach*.

The messages within that book have led to news stories, speaking engagements, podcast appearances (and more) throughout the country and the world about the dangers and impact of bullying. And yet here I was, not even aware of the level of pain my son felt. The level of pain he felt from bullying and the drastic measure he almost took.

*There but for the Grace of God.*

My son was always a big kid. He was born with neurological challenges that impacted how he walked–how he ran–and how he played.

And he was bullied.

He was bullied because he was different, AND he was bullied predominantly by adults–which we learned was not an aberration.

He was bullied by parents in our neighborhood.

When he was four years old, he heard from a neighbor, "You are TOO BIG to come inside and play with the other kids ... GO HOME!"

And it broke his heart ... and ours.

But he wasn't alone; 27% of children report being bullied by parents.

He was bullied by coaches.

"You are a detriment to the team. But I am not going to cut you. I want YOU to quit."

But again, he was not alone; 42% of children report being bullied by physical education teachers and coaches.

Teachers did not bully him; most were very helpful to Tommy. But many teachers do bully children. Thirty-seven percent of children report being bullied by teachers.

As a family, we used basketball as one tool to help Tommy learn to love the body that God had gifted him with and recognize that he, made in God's image, was truly a gift.

Through this journey, I learned so much, dealt with many of my childhood traumas, and failed forward often as we set our eyes on helping our son, helping all children–and eventually helping a community.

I learned that bullying behaviors by coaches can lead to short-term adverse impacts, e.g., an 8-year-old child being told over and over that she is not good enough and not having the opportunity to play the game she loves.

To longer-term impacts, as this same child grows into an adult who continues to believe that she is not good enough, has become risk averse, and shares how she has missed out on so much because of her fear and self-loathing.

I learned of a child who was repeatedly told by parents and coaches that she was "too fat and lazy," which deeply hurt her at the time. This led to isolation, despair, and loneliness. As an adult, she came to "hate her own body," developed an eating disorder, and experienced multiple chronic health conditions. She was eventually dismissed from her primary care doctor's practice for being a "non-compliant" patient because she didn't follow a strict exercise and diet regimen prescribed by a doctor who was unaware of the bullying and trauma this woman had experienced throughout her life.

To eternal impacts. There was a child who had bravely endured twenty-six surgeries, including the surgical placement of a colostomy bag. Despite his bravery, he was relentlessly bullied by his peers because of his medical condition. His parents tried to intervene to stop the bullying, but according to them, their actions only made things worse. Tragically, the child ended up taking his own life. Almost half a million children attempt suicide per year.

"Just toughen up" is not nearly good enough. There are short-term impacts, longitudinal impacts, and risks to children's lives.

We must do better. And we can. Together.

And thus, as our family continued to learn along our own journey, we chose to do all we could to make a difference, e.g.,

1. For the children in our community, we created an approach, a model, and a team for children (and families) seeking a loving community, where the X's and O's of coaching were important yet far less important than the love (sometimes tough-love) shared.

2. For the woman labeled "non-compliant" (and for all in our community struggling to engage the healthcare system), we ensured access to a

relationship-centered care model, where our care team shared time with her, developed relationship and mutual trust, and in this safe space heard her story, and co-created with her a personalized evidence-based pathway to healing which we walked side-by-side with her.

Throughout this journey, we also learned of the profound impact of ACES (Adverse Childhood Experiences) on children and adults.

ACES are traumatic events occurring before the age of 18. They include all types of abuse and neglect, as well as parental mental illness, substance use, divorce, incarceration, domestic violence, and the loss of a parent.

ACES include aspects of the child's environment that can undermine their sense of safety, stability, and bonding.

As a coach, and with the construct of High-Reliability Organizations (HROs) in mind, I knew I needed to learn quickly. Thus, I deferred to many experts to teach me, guide me, and mentor me as our players, our children, and our community bravely dealt with their own ACES.

- We had three children lose a parent during my coaching tenure.
- We had a child with body dysmorphia driven by his own ACES.
- We had a child who was neglected and abused at home.
- We had a child turn to drugs as he faced his own ACES.
- And many others.

With great teachers, I learned of the linkage of ACES to chronic health problems, mental illness, suicidal ideation, substance use disorders in adolescence and adulthood, and more.

I learned how common ACES are:

- 61% of adults surveyed across 25 states reported they had experienced at least one type of ACE, and

- Nearly 1 in 6 reported they had experienced four or more types of ACES.

I learned how ACES can negatively impact education, job opportunities, and earning potential. I learned that bullying has recently been added to the ACES list.

Throughout this journey and with great teachers, I learned what does not work to stop bullying, what does work, and how to help mitigate the impact of ACES in general.

Based on the evidence, what approaches have been proven to be ineffective in addressing the issue of bullying?

Below are three stop-bullying initiatives with good intentions that research has indicated have little to no impact or, in some cases, worsen the situation.

1. **Zero Tolerance Policies**

Many schools, school districts, and other programs have implemented policies requiring children who bully to be suspended or expelled.

What the research highlights is twofold:

1. *The threat of suspension or expulsion discourages children and adults from reporting bullying,* leading *to more bullying.*

2. *Punishments for minority students tend to be more severe and repercussions harsher (an awful unintended consequence of this approach)*

2. **Conflict Resolution and Peer Mediation**

These are common strategies used to address a variety of issues, and thus good-intentioned people surmised these could be helpful to stop bullying as well.

1. *Bullying is not a conflict; it is a form of victimization.*

2. *This approach sends the wrong message* to students, essentially saying, "*You are both partly right and partly wrong,*" *or "We need you two to work out this conflict between you.*"

3. *no evidence exists that conflict resolution or peer mediation stops bullying.*

3. **Group Treatment for Children**

The research highlights:

1. Group members tend to serve as role models for each other, which *typically reinforces antisocial or bullying behavior*, essentially creating a peer group for those who exhibit bullying behaviors

So, what does the evidence show that works to stop bullying?

1. Engage children (be they students, sports league players, or others) in creating the rights and responsibilities for all.

2. Peer mentors—Identify and engage high-performing, respected, loving children as "stop bullying influencers."

3. Position these children to set clear stop-bullying goals that are properly communicated to all.

4. Embrace a small test of change mindset with a solid measurement strategy — think PDSA models — and empower children to implement their ideas to stop bullying.

5. In concert, measure, analyze, and act upon the outcomes of each initiative to achieve continuous improvement. For example, celebrate successes and learn from opportunities that arise.

6. Integrate social-emotional learning (SEL) to help children understand and manage their emotions. The Five Core SEL Competencies include:

1. Self-Awareness
2. Self-Management
3. Social Awareness
4. Relationship Skills
5. Responsible Decision-Making

I also learned of the power of Positive Childhood Experiences (PCES) to mitigate the impact of bullying (and all ACES). Children who experience PCES become adults who are able to seek social and emotional support and thus will counteract the impact of ACES.

The 7 PCEs are:

1. The ability to talk with family about feelings.
2. The sense that family is supportive during difficult times.
3. The enjoyment of participation in community traditions.
4. Feeling a sense of belonging in school.
5. Feeling supported by friends.
6. Having at least two non-parent adults (e.g., coaches, teachers) who genuinely care.
7. Feeling safe and protected by an adult in the home.

Together with our community and with love in our hearts while relying on experts and evidence, we also created a model that created opportunities for these genuine and loving connections (these PCES). We sought those children we knew to be suffering to join us and heal as we sought the *what if…*

*What if…*

*What if a message of faith, hope, love, care, and communal support reaches all children — such that the idea of even thinking about what it would be like to hurt self or others that arise from painful feelings and thoughts within them never arose?*

*What if the messages of "you are enough," "you are not alone," "you are loved," "the eternal God loves you," and similar were amplified in such a way that those who could be most vulnerable and susceptible to these thoughts had their minds changed or, better yet, these thoughts never crossed their minds?*

*What if…*

Together.

**About the Author**

Named a Healthcare Disruptor and a Mental Health Champion by Authority Magazine, Tom is an internationally recognized speaker and writer focusing on leading with love, courageous vulnerability, systems thinking and improvement, stopping bullying, amplifying positive childhood experiences, and bringing "love in action" to all we do.

Tom is the former Parent Partnership program leader for the National Institute for Children's Health Quality (NICHQ). More recently, he and his team led the Michigan statewide implementation efforts of the

Collaborative Care Model for Adolescents to improve access to mental health services.

Tom is the founder of TBKID Youth Sports Programs, which ensures inclusion and belonging, promotes positive, life-changing social and emotional skills, and promotes fun and play. He was also an advisor to an island nation health system seeking to address child abuse and improve the child and family patient experience.

Tom's multiple award-winning book, *From Heart to Head & Back Again ... a journey through the healthcare system*, is a call to action serving to bring people together to make a positive impact for others in healthcare and beyond and served as a 2021 AUPHA book award for healthcare leaders of tomorrow.

Tom's multiple award-winning book, *The Big Kid and Basketball ... and the lessons he taught his Father and Coach*, focusing on bullying, ACES, and PCES, has significantly improved youth sport and school system and improved child experience and well-being.

He is a contributing author of the #1 Children's Stop Bullying book, *Brave Kids: Short Stories to Inspire Our Future World-Changers*. His forthcoming book series, *The Light* ... is already garnering much attention as it reassures children that God loves them, they are never alone, they are each empowered by the Holy Spirit and thus have His power within (agency), they are lovable, and they are loved.

Tom is a child advocate and a voice for stopping bullying and amplifying positive childhood experiences for all children. He is a parent and former athlete who became a coach to help children and communities.

At the end of the day, he truly believes love (God) is the force multiplier.

dahlborghlg.com

Tom@DahlborgHLG.com

# Chapter 6

# Compassion Is The Path

Nora D'Ecclesis

### Why is Cretin a Pejorative Term?

Cretin is a pejorative term. It is often used in the film and television industry and even by journalists to indicate low-level intelligence, with a pejorative slant and emphasis on less-than-average cognitive ability. Therefore, it trickles down to conversational derogatory slang for all levels of society who bully and humiliate.

The medical profession omitted the use of the term cretin but not the lexicon. How did this slip into the lexicon, and why wasn't it seen more recently to be as horrifically discriminatory as other similar genetic congenital diseases? Maybe because a baby is born with this condition through no fault of their own, and it can be treated depending on how early it's diagnosed. This can result in few visible signs of any problem, allowing the person to assimilate more readily into the general population. A child with this disease has no visible signs of being handicapped. It isn't until the socialization process is impaired or special classes are needed that the disease becomes more public.

The interesting thing is that so little is known about congenital thyroid disease that few young classmates refer to these youngsters using the pejorative cretin term. They simply say they are dumb kids, stupid, and call them shorty. If cretinism were routinely used to identify congenital hypothyroidism, we can only imagine how much more it would have been used in teenage bullying behaviors in the late 1960s. So, why, then, is it still being used by adults? Perhaps it is because it is now synonymous with dumb, stupid, or cognitively inferior, and it seems to cause a bit of laughter when used. In a very informal question to several adults without the benefit of a Google search, many will answer cretin equals dumb with no knowledge it came from a neonatal medical condition now more under control and treated in infancy.

The cretin term is, however, used by many adults in any general verbal attack on another human. It seems to be more fun than simply calling their adversary a dummy. Many use the word cretin if they disagree; for example, politically, journalists say, "That person running for office is a cretin!" "Why listen to the opinion of that cretin?"

## America Starts Neonatal Testing for Congenital Hypothyroidism

Prior to the early 1970s, newborn screening for congenital hypothyroidism and various other diseases was not available despite the potential for early detection and treatment. A brilliant M.D., Ph.D. American microbiologist Dr. Robert Guthrie discovered a way to prick a newborn's heel a few days after birth and then place the blood droplets on a specially designed filter paper to determine if a disease was present. So, in America in the early 1960s, this was the beginning of a new era to eradicate these horrific congenital diseases and treat them. Dr. Robert Guthrie developed this first test to screen for a disease called PKU Phenylketonuria, which resulted in mental retardation if not diagnosed. Nutritional intervention could make all the difference. A heel stick for a blood sample from the newborn after a few days was a valuable tool for diagnosis. After the heel stick, five drops of the baby's blood went onto the specially designed filter paper on what looked like an index card. Those five drops enabled physicians to diagnose and eventually treat a multitude of diseases, including congenital hypothyroidism, sickle cell disease, and PKU.

Each year, around 10,000 infants in the United States receive appropriate treatment due to these tests. Today, a more sophisticated test enhances that test called mass spectrometry. Dr. Guthrie was married to Margaret, and it was her niece who had a case of undiagnosed PKU, which acted as the inspiration for the initial research. Dr. and Mrs. Guthrie then had a son born mentally retarded, so as a microbiologist and physician, Dr. Guthrie's research continued benefitting humanity. It is important to note that it took years for the AMA to accept this testing and to set medical standards for its use. Then, the states had to accept the procedure, which took many years.

Many instances can be found where physicians are personally affected by the diseases to which they devote their time and research. Fortunately, the representatives in the American Congress and President George Bush, who signed the legislation, supported advancing the acceptance and utilization of the five drops of blood at birth.

**Causes and Consequences of Congenital Hypothyroidism**

We look now at the causes and consequences of no testing for congenital hypothyroidism and the tragic way in which it progressed in those youngsters born before the 1965-1970 diagnostic testing era.

In proximity to the 1965 testing, the only way physicians knew of the problems of insufficient thyroid in the infant was when the baby failed to thrive due mainly to one of the first symptoms, an enlarged tongue. The caregiver complained to the pediatrician that a hernia had formed and the infant had a swollen and distended abdomen. The next thing the parent or caregiver might notice is total hair loss and drooping eyelids. There is almost immediate neurological impairment, and the skin looks old at two weeks. Unfortunately, once the weeks continue in ten or more, there is some cognitive deficit and delayed bone maturation, so if dad is 6'5", even medicated, the child might be 4'11" - to, at best, 5'3". The visual and physical changes in those early years were irreversible.

If the diagnosis is incorrect, the infant will exhibit prompt abnormal bone growth, lethargy, excessive sleep, minimal crying, muscle tone floppiness, particularly in the ears, and a severely hoarse voice.

The swollen tongue and the swelling in the neck, indicating a goiter, are very obvious. One interesting and additional process is the autistic characteristics that are now being explored as an additional secondary problem if not medicated early enough with thyroid medications.

**The Most Common Cause**

There is strong evidence suggesting that congenital hypothyroidism is caused by insufficient iodine in the nutrition of parents. Early in the 20th century, congenital hypothyroidism became less common with the introduction of iodine in salt, but not in all salt, and certainly not in all countries initially. A question in 2024 that comes to mind is, as the medical profession sees salt as needing to be restricted because of hypertension, then how does the expectant mother get enough if not taking prenatal vitamins? Prevention is in the hands of multiple primary care physicians, physician assistants, midwives, and gynecologists to ensure the pregnant mother is ingesting the recommended daily allowance of iodine.

Another causative possibility is as simple as a baby born without a thyroid. The mother of the congenital hypothyroid baby might also have had radioactive iodine during pregnancy or used medications such as sulfonamides or lithium. This is also new genetic research indicating a defect in a gene that might be a causative factor.

The progress in Guthrie-type neonatal testing a day or so after a baby's birth has eliminated virtually all of the above. Of course, there are occasional false negatives, so it is now suggested that an additional test be performed 14 days after birth. Also, administering the medication to an infant until about age three is difficult, perhaps altering the prognosis toward a more negative outcome with neuro-developmental pathology.

## Etymology

So where did that cretin term come from? It is thought that early in the 1700s, the horror of seeing the poor, unmedicated congenital hypothyroid youngsters around the world, many of who were severely dwarfed and dying in childhood, that calling them by a Christian term was compassionate. In France, the word Chretien means a Christian greeting, reminding people the distorted appearance of the children should be thought of as a saint-like little creature who did not sin, but from the Latin word Cretira, meaning creature.

Is the etymology of cretinism significant? It is not at this point. Centuries ago, in the Switzerland Alps, the cretin word was defined as "one who is human despite deformities," and that can be found in Webster's dictionary. Cretin is used harshly and with great frequency in a way that is more consistent with the Latin, and it needs to be eliminated along with the other derogatory terms such as lunatic, spastic, and trisomy that have been used in the past to denote cognitive impairment or physical disability. Healthcare in America ICD-10 lists the correct medical terminology as "congenital iodine deficiency syndrome."

## The Government Steps In

On April 24, 2008, President George W. Bush signed the Newborn Screening Saves Lives Act, a bipartisan effort codifying neonatal screening and follow-up and offering grants. United States Senators Dodd, Hatch, Clinton, and Kennedy were instrumental in this long overdue bipartisan bill to enhance the quality and quantity of human life for generations to come. However, Generation Z children born between 1990 and 2010, usually from Generation X parents, have presented with more iron deficiency than previous generations, and so the work continues.

To call another human being cretin is perhaps justified by many as a colloquialism in speech. Still, more likely, the frequent use might be related to granting permission to the user the freedom to bully while using what they feel is a clever term. It is clever because it has become synonymous with the slang derogatory dumb, idiot, imbecile, and many other horrible terms with the benefit of sounding erudite. Can you imagine actually feeling so elitist that the word cretin could be replaced by Trisomy 21 in a verbal attack on the perceived human's intellectual prowess?

Neanderthals and children from the prehistoric era with congenital diseases such as Trisomy 21, having recently been reported by Spanish paleontologists, were cared for by the tribe without even an expectation of reciprocity. Their caregiving is theorized to have resulted from compassion. Cretin is a pejorative term. It is a derogatory term with no merit and should be eliminated. It is certainly not tolerated in speech that subjects anyone to humiliation. Compassion is the appropriate path.

**About the Author**

Nora D'Ecclesis is a distinguished, award-winning historical fiction and nonfiction author. She graduated from Kean University with a B.A., M.A., and LDT/C. Her early career was as an educator specializing as a certified learning disabilities consultant. Nora owns Renaissance Presentations, which offers weekend retreats with experts in meditation, equanimity, nature hikes, haiku, time management, and mindfulness. Through her books, expertise, and experiences, D'Ecclesis empowers her audience to live life more mindfully.

*The Contessa's Legacy, A Novella*, is a historical novel published in 2024 and won several book awards, including the 2024 International Impact Award for Best Historical Fiction, the Firebird Book Award, and the American Fiction Finalist Award. It has stayed in the number 1-3 bestseller spots for the first four months since publication.

www.noradecclesis.com

# Chapter 7

# The Power of Connections

Sheila Brune

I'm a huge believer in the power of connections and building connectivity between people. Whether it's health care professionals and patients or just friends and relatives, the power of connectivity cannot be underestimated.

For several years, I had become a loyal and voracious reader of obituaries in the local newspaper. I had my reasons for doing this, but as time passed, I read more and more obituaries of my patients, some of whom I had known and cared for. I was the director of case management in a mid-sized hospital in the Midwest. As I read my patients' stories after their death, I realized there were things I wished I had known about them while they were alive.

Sometimes, I had tremendous remorse and regret for the things I never knew and the connections I never made. I considered collecting the life stories of our still-alive patients. I also started exploring the importance of connecting with people and how we could make connections through the writing of stories.

In 2001, I thought about my ideas and acted upon them, and thus came the beginning of the Living History Program©, a way to create something to bring purpose to our patient's lives. I put volunteers at the bedside to ask a series of scripted questions about the person they were interviewing. Then those answers became a beautifully written story of the person's life, much like an obituary, but as a LIVING HISTORY: a story written while they were alive—a story they and their family could hopefully enjoy for years to come.

Many years later, I fully understand the true power of connectivity. I learned we connect on three different levels. Through stories, we connect on a real level. That's when we read something in the story that is a real commonality between two people. It may be something you both enjoy, something you did in your past or present life that you have in common, or just an intense feeling of connectivity through successes, failures, sadness, grief, and great happiness.

We also make connections on a compassionate level. Hearing something in the person's story gives you a deeper understanding or compassion for them. So many times in our lives, we find someone who has traveled a road so deeply full of sadness that we can only share in their pain. Those are compassionate connections. They truly touch your heart.

Finally, there are scripted connections. That's when we hear something in a person's story and discover that we want to know more about them. That is when we ask those more profound questions. "I'd like to hear more about that." It shows interest in the person and allows us to learn something new, exciting, fun, or just informational. Our own story grows as we listen with an open heart to those we care for.

I have so many stories of how we have learned to be more compassionate, caring, and loving to people just by hearing their stories. I'll share just one.

One day, a nurse approached me and asked, "Would you please do a story on my patient? This lady is so sweet, and none of us have cared for her. I know she has a story." I sent one of my trained story writers to interview her, and the story they brought back was painful, and the impact on her life was huge.

She told the story of her life as a mother of eleven children. One day, her husband said she should take the children shopping for school clothes.

She left the three youngest children at home with the three oldest children and took the five middle ones with her.

She said, "I didn't drive much in those days because I had so many children, and the roads had big curbs. I met a dump truck on a curve and ran up on that edge, throwing my car out of control and into the lane of the approaching truck. That day, three of my children were killed. I was in the hospital for three months, and of course, I was unable to attend their funerals. When I got out of the hospital, I asked my husband to help me get through my sadness." He said he thought it was better if we didn't talk about those children and we should concentrate on raising the eight remaining children. Of course, she wept, telling her story. So did the story writer.

Her story moved everyone, but the best response came from one nurse who told me, "This lady is never grumpy or demanding, but if she were, I would forgive her because of so much she's been through. I would understand."

The patient also confirmed what we always thought to be true. The patient told us how thankful she was for the opportunity to talk about her lost children. She thanked us for the story, and we sincerely thanked her for sharing it with us.

To me, this says everything that needs to be said about the power of connectivity.

In the hospital setting, writing every patient's story was impossible. However, through the process of getting stories, healthcare workers learned how to ask questions of the patient and find answers without writing a story. Some of the things we always ask are questions about family. It's important to know how many children the patient has, how many grandchildren, or maybe just the story of their pets. More importantly, we need to find out what they love and value most in their lives. Knowing their path in life, their jobs, or professions helps make connections. We need to find out what they like to do. What do they watch on television, what do they read, do they like to cook, do they like to garden? All these things are very important to us in caring for the patient.

Building connections with patients absolutely contributes to a more holistic approach to health care. We don't just know what's wrong with them physically, but we also know how they have lived and become the people they are today.

Initially, we were curious about the advantages of engaging with patients through their personal stories. We found out emphatically in the first survey of patients who had stories written while in our care. When we asked if they felt their story contributed to the quality of the health care they received during their hospitalization, they overwhelmingly replied yes! They said they knew and felt when people read their story and used it in their daily interactions. They also told us they could tell when the story hadn't been read, which made a difference in their care.

Conversations are deeper and more meaningful when you know just a little bit about someone. They become important as you learn more and hear more details of their story. Our writers often would come back from interviewing patients and say how much they loved them. One story writer always returned from an interview saying, "I just made a new friend!" Sometimes, he would say, "I just made a new BEST friend!"

We have learned to always be grateful for the opportunity to connect with the patient and discover their hidden treasures. We say thanks and tell them what a pleasure it was to meet them, hear their story, and hand over the finished story with two hands as if it were a box wrapped with a ribbon. For it is...it is a gift! It is a treasure to us, the patient, and the family.

Connectivity with a person can be a real ego burst—to have someone show interest in your life is reaffirming that you matter—and that your life is important. So many patients tell us, "I don't have much of a story" or "I'm not that interesting." We respond, "Let me be the judge of that."

So, one last story.

One lady said the usual, "I don't have a story."

We found out that was not true. She said they lived in a small town in upstate New York when she was a little girl. It was a place where many of the rich and famous from New York City would go in the summer to escape the city heat. One of those men hired her father to be a groundskeeper.

She told us that this same gentleman told ghost stories one night a week in the church basement, and sometimes he would seriously scare them. She said, "One time, he scared me so bad I fell off the stump I was sitting on."

By the end of the summer, he discovered she liked cats just as much as he did. When he left, he gave her two kittens, and she got to name them. One was Mark, and one was Twain.

Yes, she heard ghost stories from the lips of Mark Twain. The real-honest-to-God Samuel Clemens. Her son brought a big picture of his mother sitting on Mark Twain's lap. What a treasure. And what a story! Almost everyone in the Midwest could have a connection with that story. We all grew up with Tom Sawyer and Becky!

Connections **are** amazing, and everyone has a story full of them. You just need to care enough to make them happen.

## About the Author

Sheila Brune is an RN with over 50 years of experience in healthcare. She is a former director of service excellence, quality director, and risk manager. She became a passionate promoter of patient advocacy. Sheila was certified in healthcare quality and case management. She completed her Master of Science Degree in Health Services Administration from the University of

St. Francis in Joliet, Illinois, and in 2021, she was named a Distinguished Alumni. She was a regular presenter at healthcare conferences, promoting the patient experience, family involvement in healthcare, the value of excellent communication, and relationship building.

Sheila was awarded the Innovation in Patient Care Award by the Iowa Association of Nurse Leaders and the Bright Ideas Award from the Iowa Society for Healthcare Marketing and Public Relations. She was a NurseWeek finalist for the Nursing Excellence Award for Patient Advocacy. In 2001, she received an award from The American Society on Aging and Pfizer for innovation in the care of the elderly. In 2002 she received the Innovative Service Excellence Award from the Healthcare Service Excellence Association. She received the S. A. Gross Award from Illinois Provider Trust for her work in risk management. In 2016, she was awarded the Ruth Ravich Award from the Patient Advocacy Community of the Beryl Institute.

Since 2001, Sheila has shared her innovative Living History Program© program with hundreds of organizations and implemented it across the United States and Canada.

Today, she is happily retired from full-time employment. She is a substitute school nurse at an elementary school in Northwest Indiana, where she and her husband reside. With six grandchildren close by, her life is just about perfect!

livinghistoryprogram.com

sslbrune@comcast.net

# Chapter 8

## Yoga, Reiki, Awaken

Andrea L. Wehlann

After my third pregnancy, my middle son, Luka, passed away. I later experienced several miscarriages and noticed that an untreated eye infection led to swelling in my joints. It started on one side, from my ankle upwards. Since it was left untreated due to my circumstances at that time, it affected the left side of my body and, eventually, both sides. I became unable to walk. Once I could no longer navigate the staircase with my two babies, I was finally allowed to seek medical treatment. My doctor and a rheumatologist diagnosed me with reactive arthritis, rheumatoid arthritis, and autoimmune disease. I underwent injections in my joints, consulted with specialists, and was prescribed numerous medications. I was informed I would have to take these pills for life to manage future outbreaks. As a new mother who had just buried a son and with two young babies under three, I found myself repeating my mantra daily: "Be a good mom." The medications had a strong effect on my body, causing intense pain and leaving me overwhelmed and on my knees. In this space of hitting rock bottom in my marriage, motherhood, and health, I did what I knew I could. I meditated. I sat still, closed my eyes, and connected inside. I would breathe and bring attention to my breath. I could sit for moments this way and feel pain-free. Gently, I began to inhale and exhale, lengthening my breath. I used the counting breath technique: inhale for 3, exhale for 4, inhale for 4, exhale for 5, inhale for 5, exhale for 6, repeat, and then reverse. I then raised my arms above my head with each inhale, touched my hands, looked up to my thumbnails, smiled and paused, exhaled my arms wide, and looked down as I exhaled to stretch the back of my neck.

For a long time, this was all I could do. I did it because one of my heroes, Martin Luther King, taught me if you can't run, walk, and if you can't walk, crawl. Each day for months, I crawled, meditated, stretched my arms and neck, and repeated my mantra: "Be a good mom, just be a good mom." Slowly, I eliminated the pills, moved more, and fell deeper into the ease I was creating within. I added to my stretches and yoga asanas and held them longer. The inflammation was reduced with healthy diet changes and being aware of acid/alkalinity. Steroids helped bring the inflammation and swelling back to normal. Still, I believe that yoga, meditation, and the belief in my ability to heal myself without relying solely on pharmaceuticals also played a significant role in my healing.

## Yoga

Yoga can help with stress and anxiety by offering a backbone of practice and skills. One that practices its Yama's, Niyama's, of the eight limbs of yoga, creates an ethical foundation to rely on when the storms of life arise. Having tools to manage stress and anxiety deepens our sense of self, self-confidence, and self-esteem in handling difficult emotions. One technique of value in yoga is the art of concentration, whereby we use the breath (as one example) as an object for attention. Through my Buddhism and Zen studies, I learned that the mind has two functions: it forgets, and it remembers. With this technique, we practice returning our attention to the object of focus once it starts to wander. Each time we redirect our attention to the breath, we enhance our focus, awareness, and concentration. Once developed, you can apply this skill to any daily stressor. When you focus on heartbreak, stress, anxiety, or dis-ease, you can bring attention back onto a positive seed, a joyous moment. In this way, we can reduce suffering and create more moments of joy by flowing with the nature of life; just as breathing inhales and exhales, the waves of the ocean ebb and flow, and emotions arise and pass. Knowing this, we can become less stuck when more challenging emotions occur. We have something within us we have strengthened, felt, cultivated, watered, which no one else can see or take from us. Yoga is this. Yoga aligns us with this center, this kingdom we each have within us. Yoga is beyond the five senses and reveals an innate world beyond what we can see, hear, taste, and touch.

Yoga promotes the body's natural healing and boosts immunity by stretching tight areas in yoga postures. Only two or three of Patanjali's yoga sutras focus on actual physical postures out of over 200. Yet it is so essential to move the body. Energy gets stored in some places, inflames, causing dis-ease, illness, pain etc. In asana (yoga postures), we elongate muscles, tension, flexion, and bend the spine forwards and backward, all healing the body mentally, physically, and emotionally. Essentially, in asana, we create space in the body for the breath to flow into and out of. Imagine inhaling deeply to release soreness and tension in your body. Yoga is ease, effortlessness, nature, and homeostasis in the body. It is important to note the body is always trying to heal itself. When one is in a yoga class, we are essentially creating conditions for the body to heal and return to homeostasis.

Yoga postures allow space for healing, health, wealth, kindness, and compassion. Ujjayi Pranayama, a Pranayama breathing technique, is known as the cleansing breath, the ocean breath. We can heal our organs by practicing Pranayama and Asana to breathe fresh oxygen into spaces once in pain or fatigue. In this space, our immune system can thrive and renew. Our cellular patterns can elongate and rejuvenate. Mentally and emotionally, we are learning to breathe through challenges. Learning how we breathe in each posture represents a challenge. Breathing through the challenges is yoga. Yoga is a breathing practice. It's helpful to think of how you are breathing, and with yoga practice, we become aware of the breath patterns. "Are they long or short, fast or slow?"

For instance, when sitting at a computer all day, what begins to happen is the chest falls inward, and hence, our inhale comes to the top of the diaphragm only. When this happens, we receive and feel less oxygen. If we use a technique taught by my Zen Buddhist Ashtanga yoga teacher, we can learn to tilt the pelvis forward near the front of the chair, automatically highlighting the natural curve of our lumbar spine. The tips of the shoulder blades draw downward here, collarbones widen across the chest, the chest is open towards the sky, and the breath rises from the root of the pelvis up through the face and spreads beautifully across the sinuses. The exhale travels past the belly button to the center of the perineum. All of us can become aware of this natural rhythm of the breath in our body and use it to optimize our mental, physical, and immune health. The effects of more oxygen and better posture, rooting the pelvis as the roots of a tree, can be felt immediately. Therefore, healing can happen in an instant. This is how yoga becomes a backbone, a tool of consciousness we use not only on our yoga mats but in our lives, relationships, driving, families, homes, fridges, and work. Practicing yoga on your mat weekly will yield quicker results than practicing only a few times a month. The body retains every yoga practice. I have witnessed yoga students who haven't practiced for years, reached a plateau, and didn't attend for a year or so, or when life's challenges consume them. I am quick to remind them that yoga and all their practices have not left them; it is still within them. Just as muscle memory for those who lift weights, the muscles remember, the body, indeed, does keep score.

As BKS Iyengar's book, *Light of Yoga*, teaches, yoga is like a light; once lit, it cannot be dimmed. I will add that once you connect to the inner peace within you in yoga practices, being still, connecting to your breath, and experiencing beyond the five senses, it never fades. You can contact that place at any time during the day or night. Feeling this connection is empowering and can be expanded to hold moment after moment, building a meditation practice and holding space for tough emotions to arise and pass. This contributes to a healthy state of being. This contributes to remaining calm amidst the chaos.

If you are a beginner, just begin. Those are the entry points to delve into if you feel swollen, heartbroken, abandoned, alone, hungry, or craving. Follow your sensations; this is the essence of the yogic and now famous Zen saying, "Start where you are." A teacher will always guide you when you get stuck. You can practice online, yet when you have a teacher, they can see where you are and guide you to where you want to be.

## Reiki

'Rei' means Universal, and 'Ki' means Energy, or Chi is a more popular term that means Energy. Reiki healing is a hands-on healing technique using symbols to allow Universal energy to flow through the hands of the Reiki practitioner into the body of the Reiki healing recipient. Reiki can be hands-on, or practitioners can be trained to use the symbols for distant Reiki healing through ancient practices from the lineage of Dr. Mikao Usui. There is a connection between the Reiki Master and the energy felt and cultivated through the practice, use of symbols, and attunements to energetic frequencies and vibrations. As a Reiki Master for over 20 years, my practice has become almost innate and is embedded in my actions today. When I offer Reiki to those who wish to receive, it is as if the palm of my hand is an open source for the universal energy to flow through. Envision a flashlight shining through the palm of my hands to the recipient's body. I love being a Reiki Master, as I can be an empty vessel for the light. Reiki is not static; it flows and constantly moves, as all energy does. It is important to remind the patient to trust in this energetic 'Ki' and that it will go to the places and spaces within their body that need it most or need healing.

When I worked in the group homes in Toronto with adults with HIV/AIDS as a support worker, I was responsible for administering medication and assisting with their daily activities. I discovered what helped them most was when I would touch their arms and hold their hands as they passed. There was a sense of peace and calm. I watched them suffer heavily from the side effects of mostly experimental drugs. This experience led me to delve deeper into my studies and training, including meditation, yoga, Reiki, and Chi Kung. I also studied with Dr. Eric Pearl to become a reconnective healing practitioner. Through this, I discovered innate energy healing frequencies and amazing hands-off techniques developed by the chiropractor Dr. Eric Pearl as he worked with his patients.

Patients experience calm, ease, and relaxation with Reiki. This is the benefit of many healing modalities, such as yoga, Reiki, massage therapy, aromatherapy, etc.

At this point, the body shifts in the nervous system, moving from the sympathetic to the parasympathetic nervous system. The body's healing capacities are minimal when in constant frozen or flight mode. As I learned from studying metaphysics, the mind cannot serve two masters. Therefore, if we are not in a state of peaceful rest and healing, we are filled with pain, stress, and disease. For the body to heal itself, we must be and create the conditions for such a state. This is where yoga and Reiki can help to provide conditions for the body and mind to heal.

Many Western medications, surgeries, and treatment plans do not include these. My yoga students from India who attend my studio, Ganga Moon Yoga, have told me that when they visit the doctor for an issue, they are given a few yoga poses to practice as part of their treatment. Hearing this warms my heart. It's beautiful to see how we can truly heal ourselves.

I often remind my yoga students, "You are more than your thoughts" and "You are more than you think you are." Think big and dream big. There is greatness within you now.

**About the Author**

Andrea L. Wehlann is the Founder & CEO of Ganga Moon Yoga and Reiki Skool. She holds a BA in psychology from Brock University and a social services diploma from Niagara College. Andrea has extensive experience in the social services field and is a Reiki Master, Brazilian Jiu Jitsu, Chi Kung, Feng Shui, and meditation teacher. She is also the author of three books: the bestseller *Deeper Days: 365 Yoga-spirations for Inner Calm Amidst Chaos, No Matter How Dark the Stain: Poems and Inspiration for the Woman in Pain*, and the bestseller *Stillness in the Storm: A Conscious Daily Journal of Yoga and Spiritual Healing*.

ganga-moon-yoga.square.site

gangamoonyoga@gmail.com

# Chapter 9

## Connecting the Dots

Melissa Crook

The month I turned 50 and was two weeks into our latest move to Lubbock, Texas, I ended up in the emergency room twice over ten days with various symptoms, including a racing heartbeat, sky-high blood pressure, and a bladder control issue. Following extensive testing and consultation with a cardiologist, it was concluded that aside from hormonal changes associated with menopause, there were no significant physical abnormalities. There was, however, an issue with anxiety, codependency, performing and producing for approval, intrusive thoughts around health, and no peace or contentment in my life despite my then very faith-based life.

Thus began my journey in connecting the dots to how unprocessed, denied, stuffed, dissociated feelings and emotions directly affect our physical health and emotional and spiritual peace. Throughout my healing journey since the fall of 2019, I have gained valuable knowledge I wish to share with other women. By sharing, I hope they can find inspiration to embark on their own path to good health, contentment, and well-being. I want them to avoid the mistakes I made and adopt healthy practices to avoid finding themselves in a situation similar to the one I experienced.

This is why I established The Embracing Layers Network. It encompasses "The FEEL Podcast," a podcast for women focused on empowerment, embracing layers, and the journey towards living unapologetically.

It also includes The Embracing Layers Internet Radio Show and our newly released book, "Embracing Layers Unapologetically."

I am frustrated with conventional Western medicine and how many of my self-care providers, all of whom were women themselves, missed the mark on helping me connect the dots regarding what was happening in my body. Each symptom was treated in isolation as its own, with little to no discussion (unless I brought it up) about how these things could be connected. I had never heard the word perimenopause until I was several years into it. I started noticing shifts in my anxiety levels, acid reflux, and estrogen levels, with no discussion that I might be in perimenopause.

Western medicine excels in trauma care and emergency treatment, but it often falls short in addressing mental, emotional, and physical health holistically, especially in the case of women. The automatic response is to immediately medicate a symptom rather than investigate its underlying causes and find a solution. It is a reactive versus proactive approach.

We must see a marriage between holistic, functional, and traditional Western medicine. Sometimes, a prescription or surgery is necessary, but let's explore all the options first. We must also remove pharmaceutical and insurance companies' influence on Western medicine doctors' practices. The current situation involves significant money, impacting the quality of relationships between patients and doctors and affecting the overall healthcare experience. Pharmaceuticals and health insurance have a place in the conversation but should not dictate it.

Initially, I just trusted my doctors and did whatever they told me to do for myself and my children. It wasn't until one of my children had a health condition that stumped the doctors, along with my mother-in-law's doctor initially dismissing her, when she suspected (and was later proven correct) that her breast cancer had returned. The doctors wanted to postpone treatment for another six months. If she had not insisted on a biopsy, her tumor would have had six more months to grow, and who knows if she would have been able to beat it again a second time. With our child, we got to a stage where our doctors seemed to give up or suggested that we might be overreacting. However, we persisted, and finally, when she was 20 years old, we found answers from a functional medicine doctor. He helped her heal for the first time in her life. This was also when I was dismissed for symptoms I was having. Those factors combined compel me to consistently question and seek answers, solutions, and alternatives, as I am more familiar with what's normal for my body than anyone else. Doctors do not know everything. Medicine is a practice, and it's okay to challenge and trust your intuition when something feels wrong. It's entirely acceptable to switch practitioners and seek out those who will actively listen to you, welcome your questions, and encourage your curiosity, regardless of how long you've seen that individual.

One important thing I've learned from working with functional medicine practitioners is that if several of your markers in your yearly blood work are at the high end of "normal" or the low end of "normal," it's not healthy. This means these areas are not in the median health range, and something is not functioning optimally. Over time, this could lead to health issues. Also, women of all ages need to get their blood work checked yearly. Traditional Western practitioners rarely order necessary blood work when addressing health concerns, or they may say, "Your blood work is normal," and stop asking further questions. That's when you need to consider if you're at the high or low end of "normal," if other areas need to be tested, or ask your doctor what you should do to get these low or high ends to a more normal reading. This might require finding a healthcare provider open to exploring other factors and addressing how to bring your readings to a more balanced and healthy level.

I did not know this about blood work ranges until my child's functional medicine healthcare practitioner told us eight years ago. He ran other tests that she had never done before. It made sense once he explained the logic behind too many high or low-end normal readings and why that led to trouble. However, conventional medical practitioners often emphasize the "normal" range without considering the possibility of alternative perspectives or additional factors.

Some of this had to do with our health insurance not covering these other alternative tests, so they didn't even present us with the option. We were fortunate enough to have the resources to pay for our daughter's care and supplements with the new practitioner, even though it meant maxing out more than one credit card. Our insurance did not cover most of the expenses, so over a 2-3-year period, it cost us several thousand dollars. Unfortunately, this is not feasible for most people. That's just unacceptable. In the spring of 2020, she tested healthy for the first time, four years after finally getting the help needed from the functional health practitioner. Knowing that we would not have been able to make this possible for her without the monetary resources makes me sick to think about. Many people can't do this for their children and loved ones, which is not something anyone should ever face.

A close friend who had heard about this practitioner from another friend introduced us to this functional health practitioner. My friend was looking for treatment for her autoimmune disease and her daughters, as they were not receiving adequate care from their conventional doctors. We have referred other people to this practitioner as well. Share with others when you find someone who meets your needs.

It also became apparent that it is essential to prioritize your mental and emotional health care. When you're feeling unwell and no one can explain why, it's common to experience fear, anxiety, depression, anger, and sadness. Seeking therapy can help you address and learn how to manage these feelings. Additionally, it can assist you in connecting the dots between your mental and physical health. Unfortunately, we didn't realize this early on, and as a result, we missed the opportunity to get the mental health support our child and I needed while navigating our health journeys.

Here are my final few takeaways. First, don't be afraid to ask questions. If you are not getting the answers you need, or your questions are not welcome, it's okay to find a practitioner willing to listen to and partner with you. Second, trust your inner voice and inner knowing, and follow that lead. Too often, I allowed the doctors to be the "expert" when I knew something wasn't right or more information could be had. Also, trust that you know your body better than anyone else. Trust that your loved ones and family members you may be supporting are knowledgeable about the situation, and encourage them to openly share information and ask questions without hesitation. Offer to be another ear or voice in the room if they have a visit they're concerned about.

So many times, we think we must navigate these things on our own, when most of the time, people in your life are willing to help if you simply ask them. If you are being gas-lit in any way by anyone in healthcare, that is probably not someone you want to work with. The most effective practitioners I've collaborated with possess five key qualities: exceptional intelligence, active listening skills, genuine empathy, curiosity, and a humble confidence. And yes, it is possible to be both confident and humble. That does not have to be a contradictory statement.

The last big takeaway from my experience is to make those connections between your mental, emotional, physical, and spiritual health, as well as your sexual health. They all feed off each other, and their impacts are interconnected. Be mindful of how you are fueling your body in all aspects of your life. Take the time to seek out a healthcare community genuinely interested in working with you, hearing from you, and supporting you in addressing all these areas. It is essential to have trust with your practitioners, and trust goes both ways. You are worthy of the time and effort to have high-quality care, no matter your age, identity, or economic standing, so don't tolerate anything less.

**About the Author**

Melissa Crook resides in Central California. She loves her family and the outdoors, is a huge sports fan, and is passionate about and believes in justice, mercy, equality, and empathy for ALL.

Melissa, the visionary behind The Embracing Layers Network, is not only the host of "The F.E.E.L Podcast" but also the driving force behind "The Embracing Layers Radio Show." On September 4th, 2024, the book *Embracing Layers Unapologetically* was launched. This book encapsulates the compelling content from the first four seasons of the podcast, offering readers a deep dive into embracing life's complexities with unapologetic authenticity.

embracinglayers.com.

# Chapter 10

## Medical Encounters for Youth with Autism Spectrum Disorder

Lisa Jacovsky

Youth with Autism Spectrum Disorder (ASD) often face some similar challenges during a medical appointment. The most common issue is difficulty with communication. Many children with ASD have trouble expressing their needs, understanding medical terminology, or responding to questions. This can make interactions with healthcare providers challenging. The way I describe this issue is that for a child with ASD, it is almost like they don't understand our language. Think of it as if you went to another country where you don't understand or speak the language. It can be frustrating. It can look like the child ignores the individual when, really, they don't understand. Sometimes, it can lead to tantrums from frustration as well. The child is not being naughty or bad; they are just upset because they don't understand.

Individuals with ASD may exhibit restricted interests and repetitive behaviors, benefiting from routine and structure. However, these traits can lead to distress in unfamiliar environments, causing anxiety and difficulty cooperating during medical exams or procedures.

A third major issue relates to sensory challenges. Sensitivities to lighting, noise, clothing, and temperature can cause discomfort and increased stress in medical settings. In addition, people may not realize that challenging behaviors, such as tantrums or destructive behaviors, can be driven by fear.

The individual may experience a fight-or-flight reaction if a situation is unfamiliar. In any uncomfortable situation, our initial instinct is often to leave. However, we can communicate that. An individual with ASD is redirected using verbal cues when attempting to leave, which can be overwhelming and scary. That is when behaviors and emotions become heightened. Their conduct is often misconstrued as displaying a higher level of strength than it actually possesses.

Communication and focus play a crucial role in this issue. If someone cannot focus, their short-term memory won't absorb and remember information. When they need that information for a new task, it can lead to challenging behaviors. Many of the difficulties faced by individuals with ASD are interconnected.

**Healthcare Providers**

Healthcare providers can do several things to better communicate with and support youth with ASD during medical encounters. The first is to simplify communication. You can do this by using one or two words rather than phrases. Depending on the individual, using clear, concise language and visual aids to explain procedures and instructions can also be helpful.

If possible, establish a routine. Maintain a consistent routine during visits to provide predictability and comfort. Sensory-friendly activities or objects can enhance the environment. Minimize sensory stimuli, such as bright lights and loud noises, to reduce discomfort.

Being patient and flexible is crucial. Allow extra appointment time and be flexible with procedures to accommodate the child's needs.

Maintain an open conversation with the caregivers. Work closely with caregivers who can provide insights into the child's preferences and effective communication methods. The caregiver can provide insight into the individual. They could have some other strategies to make things smoother for everyone.

If the individual is high-functioning, it's important to involve them in the visit as much as possible. Recognize that they may struggle with a lack of control. One way to build trust and respect is to ask for their opinion before turning to the caregiver. Even if the caregiver's decision ultimately prevails, seeking input from the individual beforehand is essential.

Use positive reinforcement to reward cooperation and bravery. Simple praise, stickers, or small rewards can be very effective. Acknowledge and celebrate small achievements to build the child's confidence and trust.

**Best Practices for Healthcare Providers**

- **Gradual Exposure:** For children with extreme anxiety, consider scheduling multiple short visits to acclimate them to the medical environment and procedures gradually. During these visits, practice using desensitization techniques. These can include letting the child handle medical instruments or sit in the exam chair without undergoing any procedures initially.

- **Ongoing Training:** Ensure that all staff members, including receptionists, nurses, and administrative staff, receive training on ASD and how to interact effectively with children with ASD.

- **Awareness of Triggers:** Be aware of common triggers for children with ASD and have strategies in place to manage them. It's best to customize this for those who work closely with them.

- **Modeling Behavior:** Demonstrate procedures on a doll or the child's caregiver to show what will happen next. Seeing the procedure first will help decrease anxiety and allow the individual to understand expectations.

**Primary Caregivers**

Primary caregivers can employ specific strategies to help prepare young individuals with ASD for upcoming medical appointments. For these appointments, a sensory kit can help the individual know what to expect and find comfort in the routine. This sensory kit can include items like noise-canceling headphones, fidget toys, weighted blankets, or a favorite soft toy.

A visual transition schedule is helpful for those who struggle with communication or have trouble understanding. Social stories can help children grasp the sequence of events and prepare for what to expect during a visit. The transition schedule visually outlines the current and subsequent activities, which can be helpful for individuals with ASD who may experience anxiety because of uncertainty about the duration of an activity or what follows. This tool also provides advance notice of appointments, and incorporating a countdown can further assist individuals in anticipating the visit.

If it's not possible to visit the medical facility in advance, having a book with pictures and videos of the facility can be helpful.

Another idea is incorporating familiar aspects of the child's routine into the visit. Bring their favorite snack, drink, or a familiar object that provides comfort. You can also add a calming activity or routine after the visit to help the child decompress and return to their normal routine. These are all great things to add to a PECS (picture exchange communication system) or a transition visual schedule.

For emergency room visits, have an information sheet ready with the child's medical history, medications, sensory sensitivities, and communication preferences. Call the ER in advance to inform them of the child's needs, if possible. Some hospitals have protocols for accommodating children with ASD. Make sure to bring the child's sensory kit and any comforting things to help them relax in a stressful setting.

## Technology

Many promising innovations or technologies could improve the medical experience for youth with ASD.

- **VR Exposure Therapy:** Virtual reality can simulate medical environments and procedures. This allows children to experience and become familiar with them in a controlled and safe manner. It can help reduce anxiety and prepare them for actual visits.
- **AR Apps:** Augmented reality apps can provide interactive experiences that explain medical procedures visually and engagingly. This may help children with ASD understand what will happen during their visit.
- **Sensory Management Wearables:** Devices such as noise-canceling headphones or wearable vests that provide deep pressure can help manage sensory input. These can reduce overstimulation during medical visits. Weighted blankets and backpacks are also available.
- **Biofeedback Devices:** Wearables that monitor heart rate and other physiological responses can also help. They can help caregivers and medical professionals identify when a child is becoming anxious, allowing them to intervene early.
- **Speech-Generating Devices (SGDs):** These devices can help non-verbal children or those with limited verbal skills communicate their needs and responses during medical visits. An example would be the app PROLOQUO. One simply needs to tap specific icons to have them speak the desired words.
- **Picture Exchange Communication System (PECS):** Apps and electronic versions of PECS can facilitate communication by allowing children to use pictures to express their needs and

feelings. An example would be a picture book. Individuals point to a picture of what they want to say or do or can pick out a specific image that describes their needs.

- **Calming and Relaxation Apps:** Apps that provide guided meditations, calming music, and relaxation exercises can help children manage anxiety before and during medical appointments.

- **Telehealth Services:** Telehealth can be particularly beneficial for children with ASD, as it allows them to receive medical consultations from the comfort of their homes. This can reduce the stress associated with in-person visits.

- **Remote Monitoring Tools:** Tools that allow remote monitoring of vital signs and other health metrics can reduce the need for frequent hospital visits, making healthcare more accessible and less disruptive.

- **Customized Sensory Rooms in Hospitals:** Some hospitals create sensory-friendly spaces with calming lights, sounds, and activities to provide a haven for children with ASD during medical visits.

- **Robotics:** Therapeutic robots, like the NAO robot, are being used to interact with children with ASD. These robots can provide comfort and distraction during medical procedures.

**Examples of Technologies and Innovations**

- **Floreo:** This app uses VR to create immersive experiences for children with ASD. It helps them practice social and daily living skills, including navigating medical environments.

- **Autism Glass Project:** This project uses Google Glass to provide real-time social cues and feedback to children with ASD. This helps them understand social interactions better, which can be applied in medical settings.

- **SoundEar3:** A device that visually displays noise levels. This will help manage sensory environments in waiting rooms and examination areas by keeping a comfortable noise level for children with ASD.

## Finding a Provider

For various reasons, some families might encounter difficulties finding a provider.

### 1. Lack of Specialized Training

- **Inadequate Training for Providers:** Many healthcare providers lack specialized training in managing and treating patients with ASD. This can lead to misunderstandings and inadequate care.

- **Limited Experience:** Some providers may have limited experience working with children with ASD. This can affect their ability to provide effective and compassionate care.

### 2. Access to Care

- **Geographical Barriers:** Access to specialized care can be limited, especially in rural or underserved areas. This then forces families to travel long distances for appropriate care.

- **Long Waiting Lists:** Specialized clinics and providers often have long waiting lists, delaying essential care and interventions. There is a shortage of specialists trained in ASD in certain states and regions.

**3. Financial Constraints**

- **High Costs:** Specialized care for children with ASD can be expensive, and insurance may not cover all services.

- **Insurance Limitations:** Some insurance plans may have limited coverage for therapies and interventions specifically designed for children with ASD.

**4. Coordination of Care**

- **Fragmented Services:** Families must navigate a complex web of healthcare providers, therapists, and specialists, leading to fragmented and uncoordinated care.

- **Lack of Integrated Care Models:** There is often a lack of integrated care models that address the comprehensive needs of children with ASD, including medical, behavioral, and developmental aspects. Families often struggle to find the help and support they need to locate specialists and understand the resources for their child.

**5. Stigma and Misunderstanding**

- **Stigma:** Families may face stigma or judgment from healthcare providers who do not understand ASD. This can lead to negative experiences and reluctance to seek care.

- **Misunderstanding of ASD:** Misconceptions about ASD can lead to inappropriate recommendations or interventions that do not meet the child's needs.

Navigating medical encounters can be particularly challenging for youth with ASD, as these experiences often trigger sensory sensitivities, communication barriers, and social anxieties. However, by fostering understanding and collaboration among healthcare providers, families, and youth, we can pave the way for more positive and empowering medical experiences. As we continue to advocate for inclusive, patient-centered care, we must remember that each encounter is an opportunity for growth, understanding, and enhanced quality of life. By equipping families with knowledge and tools, promoting awareness among medical professionals, and championing the voices of those on the spectrum, we can transform medical encounters from daunting challenges into affirming moments of connection and trust.

### About the Author

Lisa Jacovsky is a Psychology professor at Union College of NJ and SNHU. Lisa began writing short stories when she was seven years old. Writing is a passion for her and one of the many things she enjoys. She is currently the author of the award-winning first four books in the *Let's Talk! Series, Rascal Cat Brothers, Purrrfect as I Am,* and *Spooky Ooky Dance Party.* Lisa lives in New Jersey, where she enjoys spending time with family and friends, traveling, and working on her next books. Keep up with her on social media to see what is coming next.

Diverseinkbooks.my.canva.site

lisa@lisajay.net

### Resources for Guardians

1. **Children's book authors**: Sivan Hong, Dawn Menge, Tom Tracey Jr.

2. **Facebook groups**: Look up ASD Facebook support groups. There will always be groups specific to your state.

3. **State ASD groups—for example, NJ Autism** is amazing. I have

worked with them and highly recommend them.

4. **The National Autistic Society:** Provides practical tips for preparing for medical appointments.
    - The National Autistic Society: Health
5. **American Academy of Pediatrics (AAP):** Offers guidance on preparing children with ASD for medical visits.
    - AAP Preparing for Healthcare Visits
6. **YouTube Channels:** Many professionals and organizations create video content to help children with ASD understand medical visits.
    - Sesame Street and Autism

# Chapter 11

## Be the President of Your Health

Amber Tresca

When I was 16 and starting my junior year in high school, I noticed blood in my stool. The first healthcare provider I saw was in the emergency department at the local hospital. The doctor took a history and palpated my abdomen. I didn't undergo any tests, and the doctor did not perform a rectal exam. They sent me home with some antibiotics and told me I had "intestinal flu." A stool sample was ordered, and we dropped it off a few days later.

Soon after, I saw a pediatrician who referred me to a gastroenterologist. Before meeting with me at the office, the first thing they wanted to do was a colonoscopy. By this time, I had constant diarrhea. It was always bloody, and at times it was only blood. I remember doing nothing but going between my bedroom and the bathroom, all day and night.

When my gastroenterologist came in to speak with me after the colonoscopy, he said the inside of my colon resembled raw hamburger. He diagnosed me with ulcerative colitis (a form of inflammatory bowel disease, or IBD). I was admitted to the hospital, where I stayed for over a month. I was treated with prednisone and sulfasalazine, which was what was available in 1989. We talked about surgery, but eventually, the bleeding stopped. I had a few more serious flare-ups, another one where I was hospitalized for another month, and a few times when I refused to be hospitalized because I was a teenager. Instead, I stayed home on high doses of prednisone.

Between the ages of 18 and 25, I stayed out of the hospital. But I never achieved remission. I didn't always have diarrhea, but I had fevers and fatigue, and keeping weight on was a struggle. For a while, I didn't have health insurance and was paying out-of-pocket for my medications and doctor visits.

I completed my Bachelor's Degree in Science from Michigan State University, met my husband, and we moved to Stamford, Connecticut. It was at that point that I got health insurance. I saw a new gastroenterologist, and one of the first things he did was schedule another colonoscopy. At that colonoscopy, he told me my colon was in bad shape and recommended surgery. When the biopsies came back, they showed dysplasia. We decided on the 2-step j-pouch surgery. I was 26.

After my surgeries, I realized how little I knew about ulcerative colitis and how dangerous that was. I wasn't an active and informed patient. I began to get involved with the IBD community online to see other patients' challenges. I learned the effects of IBD go far beyond the gastrointestinal system. The belief was that these conditions only had an impact on digestion. But in recent decades, there has been a surge in research on how IBD can impact the entire body.

At the heart of IBD is inflammation. Inflammation anywhere in the body affects more than just one system, and that's certainly true with IBD. There are a host of other conditions that are connected to IBD that are called extra-intestinal manifestations. Some of them include anemia, arthritis, eye disease, kidney disorders, liver disease, skin conditions, and osteopenia/osteoporosis. People with IBD may be at a greater risk for certain types of cancers, either connected to the disease itself (such as colon cancer) or as an effect of the inflammatory process.

However, besides the physical issues, people with IBD are also more likely to live with mental health conditions, most commonly anxiety and depression. It's usually talked about as a bi-directional relationship: the IBD may lead to developing a mental health issue, and the mental health issue can negatively affect the IBD.

On top of these clinical challenges, there are also personal ones. IBD affects finances because of the high burden the disease places on our time, keeping us from work or school. It's also an expensive disease, as newer treatments coming to the market are more effective but also cost more.

The symptoms of IBD can have a significant impact on our personal lives. Family and friends may become exhausted as we navigate between periods of active disease and remission. Our energy levels may not match our peers, leading to frustrations in our interpersonal relationships. IBD truly does affect the whole person, although, in the public consciousness, it tends to be closely tied to the symptom of diarrhea (which not everyone with IBD experiences). Educating people about the wide-ranging effects of the condition is an ongoing process.

In my first experiences with the healthcare system, I received an incorrect diagnosis and inadequate treatment. The assumption was made that a serious illness would not have afflicted me, given my young age. Yet, IBD is common, especially in the area I lived in as a child and teen, and I had the classic symptoms of ulcerative colitis. My age seemed to be the most important status, not what I relayed to the healthcare providers around me.

That continues even to this day when I am referred for testing that is appropriate for someone with longstanding IBD but might not be for someone my age who doesn't live with an inflammatory condition. I've advocated for myself more than once with gatekeepers outside of the gastrointestinal community, who question my need for screening for certain types of cancer or other conditions.

I regularly encounter stories within the IBD community of people who have received a misdiagnosis. Nearly everyone has had a lengthy journey to diagnosis, often involving being misdiagnosed or enduring a prolonged wait for a colonoscopy or other diagnostic tests. In my case, the healthcare system impeded my diagnosis and treatment. Although I received treatment for flare-ups after being diagnosed, when I aged out of my parent's insurance, I found myself in a coverage gap while in college and shortly after. While there are now protections to help young people and others get insurance, this doesn't always fully resolve the issue.

I have also been subject to fail-first practices and copay accumulators. The insurance company refused to allow me to have the treatments my healthcare team prescribed and wanted to start me on a therapy that would not work in my case. Only after many months of waiting and appealing did I finally get access to the treatment that would help me.

Treatments and preventive care are expensive, and the insurance company uses copay accumulators, which makes my out-of-pocket costs go far beyond the deductible (which I meet every year). I require regular blood tests, MRIs, and endoscopies, along with other screenings and appointments with my healthcare providers. It comes at a cost and has financially affected my family and me.

I wish I had better understood the progressive nature of IBD and that it would never leave me. I wish I had known that I had a right to ask for better treatment and to demand it. I didn't have to settle for ongoing symptoms.

And this is still true for patients today. We don't have to settle for symptoms that ruin our quality of life. We can demand more from our healthcare teams and find a way to meet our treatment goals and reach our goals in life. I advocate for myself by questioning everything. I also push back on things I don't think make sense. If there's a test I disagree with, I'll ask for an alternative. When the care costs get too high, I let my team know so we can adjust or find a different way.

I am often the educator, teaching people in the healthcare system who know little about IBD or who don't know about the surgeries I've had. I also go back to administration and senior staff members to encourage them to better prepare their staff for patients like me because I'm not that uncommon.

Even now, however, there are times I don't understand how to help myself! I know I need to be proactive about everything. I treat my IBD like a business. I make appointments, follow up on them, and keep the lines of communication open with my providers. If I don't understand something, I ask how I can learn more. I stay informed by reading and engaging with others in the IBD community, including patients, clinicians, and care partners.

Becoming an educated patient can be tricky because information surrounds us, but it's not always of high quality. Patients should start by asking their medical team where to go for information. After that, it's good to seek academic institutions such as IBD centers, which often have information online for their patients that can usually be trusted. Government sources are also helpful, and while they may not be as thorough, they may point to deeper information in peer-reviewed journals.

Reading research may seem intimidating, but individuals can learn how to navigate it. Seeking help from a gastroenterologist or another healthcare professional to comprehend research papers is also a viable approach. Plus, learning from peers is always going to yield new information. We all have to contextualize peer-to-peer conversations because everyone's experience with the disease or treatments will differ. However, we can share so much lived experience about dealing with the healthcare system, insurance companies, and personal relationships, making the journey a little easier.

In the IBD space, we need more healthcare providers to be trained on how to recognize the symptoms of IBD. You can't look at a person and assume they can't have an IBD because of their age or ethnicity, yet that happens regularly. IBD is common, and the way to diagnose it (through endoscopy) is clear. Yet, people are sometimes not referred to a gastroenterologist until they are quite ill, simply because they don't fit some profile. We also need better access to treatments across the board. Some IBD therapies are prohibitively expensive. Yet, expenses shouldn't limit whether a person can access treatment that is right for them.

The IBD community is so amazing! Many patient advocacy groups and individuals make themselves available to help other patients and their families through the ups and downs of these diseases. However, we can always do more. We can, individually and collectively, demand more from researchers, advocacy groups, pharmaceutical companies, insurance companies, and our healthcare teams. It's important to keep pointing out unmet needs and asking for ways to meet them. IBD patients often learn to "make do," but we must start looking for better access to care for ourselves and our families.

My main objective is for patients to realize that obtaining knowledge about their health is absolutely crucial. We need to do our part to ensure that we know our bodies and diseases because we are the president of our health. Our well-being concerns everyone around us, from our families to our healthcare team. They are members of our cabinet, and they can advise us, but as patients, we must make the ultimate decisions after taking in all the information we can.

## About the Author

Amber is an IBD patient (diagnosed with ulcerative colitis in 1989) who has been writing and editing patient-facing content for the IBD community since 2000, both for major online outlets and on her own site, AboutIBD.com. After ten years of active disease, medical therapy failed, and she underwent the 2-step j-pouch surgery (removal of the large intestine and creation of an internal pouch from the last part of the small intestine). In 2017, she began the "About IBD Podcast" to educate people living with IBD about their disease and to bring awareness to the patient journey. She is a speaker, facilitator, and advocate for people with IBD and a freelance writer and editor for medical websites and publications.

aboutibd.com

amber@aboutibd.com

# Chapter 12

# Laughter is the Best Medicine ... For Nurses

Mary Frances Fisher

My auspicious career in nursing and subsequent humorous events began while I attended nursing school in Toledo, Ohio, in the 1970s. In bygone days of nursing, our uniforms included nursing caps fastened with white bobby pins. Meal breaks involved an unusual route to the cafeteria—via the Emergency Room. This served a dual purpose by weeding out unsuccessful medical candidates if you tossed your lunch en route. Considering these brief facts, here is a memory best described as a perfect example of Murphy's Law.

Navigating my first few weeks in nursing school, I did my best to be inconspicuous, adhering to the principle of going with the flow. Regretfully, my flow was akin to a tsunami. Acclimating to the sight of severed limbs and copious bleeding from head wounds before ingesting food, I made my way to the cafeteria. After making my food selections, I brought my tray over to a table with fellow nursing students. I attempted to open a ketchup packet, stubbornly resisting "tear here" instructions. I finally managed to open it slightly, but nothing came out, so I squeezed it with all my might, and, voila, ketchup came spewing out like a volcano gushing lava. Unfortunately, it didn't have the courtesy of landing on my plate. Oh, heck no. It found a home in my nursing instructor's brilliant white uniform. She looked at me in disbelief, her lovely outfit giving her the appearance of a nosebleed without the sense to wait for a tissue. To say I was mortified would be an understatement.

I raced into the bathroom and was immediately hit with a stench so powerful I longed for a gas mask. I thought, not a problem. I'll grab supplies and exit in no time before someone thinks the rank odor belonged to me. Fifteen seconds later, provisions in hand, I heard a knock on the door. Assuming a nurse forgot her bathroom key, I opened the door wide, intent on making a fast exit. But avoiding embarrassment was not in the cards for me. Standing before me were three men (one was an extremely handsome man I'd seen earlier, and he gave me "the look." Although he was now giving me quite a different look.)

"We're the maintenance crew here to inspect the bathroom."

With no way to escape or provide a believable explanation, I slunk past them and practically raced down the hall. When I was a few feet away, I heard "Whoo-ee" loud enough to alert the coast guard. I wondered, could this day get any worse?" Why yes, it could and did.

I stopped for a can of club soda and brought the items to my instructor to clean her faux nosebleed (aka, ketchup). I tripped but managed to right myself. I thought, hah, something's going right after all. But I didn't realize the can was jostled in my near-tumble. Opening it resulted in an explosion of soda that gushed straight upward like a geyser with sufficient force to knock my nurse's cap off my head. By now, you've probably guessed where it landed . . . in my instructor's food. For some reason, she didn't want my help to clean up the ketchup debacle.

My hair and face were dripping with soda, and a return trip to the bathroom was necessary. Inching slowly toward the restroom, I ran into the three maintenance men as they exited. Seeing my bedraggled appearance, they burst out laughing. The attractive man I once admired had lost interest in me amidst the chaotic events. And, yep, the stench remained. Some days, you can't catch a break.

My first job as a newly minted Registered Nurse at the main campus of the Cleveland Clinic involved working on the VIP ward. Assuming my assignment involved some type of vascular ward, I was unclear what the VIP acronym meant.

I approached the nurse in charge of orientation to clarify. "Excuse me, but could you please tell me what type of unit VIP refers to?"

"It stands for Very Important People [yes, I felt incredibly stupid], and you'd be catering to famous actors, politicians, and other celebrities."

On that prestigious floor, I cared for many rich and famous people. From the variety of cases assigned to me, there is still one that makes me smile to this day.

I was caring for a member of the Saudi royal family, and his oldest son had a crush on me. We went on a few dates within walking distance of the Clinic. But I didn't assign any importance to our brief encounters—after all, he lived over seven thousand miles away. On his father's discharge day, I entered the room with a collection of various documents.

"Hi, I'm here to provide you with home-going instructions." Before I could say anything else, his son interrupted me.

He looked meaningfully at his father, who nodded before the son spoke. The words he uttered completely caught me off guard. "I would like you to be my wife."

Shocked, my head filled with thoughts of being a princess—power and wealth were in my grasp. Or, so I thought. Before I could respond, he completed the terms of his proposition. "You would be my first wife, and the most important thing is that you will rule over all other wives to follow."

My feeling of a storybook ending flew out of my head as I considered my counter-proposal. "I will be your first wife," smiles all around with high fives until I finished my response, "if you will be my first husband." To say they were displeased would be an understatement. I firmly believe they would have tossed me out the window for my temerity. Fortunately for me, the windows didn't open. My only consolation is that I lived to tell this delightful tale. I suppose being a princess wasn't meant for me.

***

After my RN status at the Cleveland Clinic's VIP ward began to lose its luster, I transitioned into routine, everyday nursing care. When dealing with a variety of patients, I had to learn the art of "keeping it real."

What's that you ask? Here's an example. I'd just arrived for my 3 to 11 PM shift, prepared to receive updated patient reports from the prior shift. Leaving the nurse's station with patient notes from the earlier shift, I felt completely professional and overly confident. Reviewing my shift report updates, I checked on my first patient, who underwent surgery two days earlier.

Calmly, I asked: "Have you experienced any flatulence today?"

In response to my mastery of medical terminology, his reply was teeming with frustration. "Why do all you nurses use such big words? No one can understand what you're talking about."

Without losing a beat, since I clearly overwhelmed him with my nursing superiority, I replied in a self-deprecating manner: "I apologize for the confusion. So, did you fart today?" His wife and another nurse laughed so hard that they had to leave. The patient nodded, unable to speak, as his face turned a bright shade of scarlet. I had my answer through my newly acquired art of keeping it real.

Testing the theory that laughter is the best medicine, I'd like to relay an amusing story about nursing skills called "Stuck at Work." After receiving the shift report, my supervisor advised I'd be transferred to another floor because they were short-staffed. Although it sounds like an easy request, being unfamiliar with patients, routines, and supplies can cause unfortunate accidents. Although you may believe a normal slip-and-fall ensued, nothing could be further from the truth.

I had just removed an IV bag from a patient and placed it on the medication counter. Reaching overhead for more supplies, I felt a piercing sensation. I didn't realize the countertop was sticky, and looking down, I was mortified to discover the needle from the IV bag pierced the left side of my stomach. It's an indescribable sight to see a needle protruding from your body, knowing that if you dared to move, you'd be dragging an IV bag with tubing on your journey. Hoping to avoid humiliation (insert laugh here), I quickly removed the offending needle to keep my secret safe. Unfortunately, when I extracted the needle, my left abdomen immediately swelled, and it was impossible to hide my seven-month-pregnancy-sized abdomen. When this grotesque abnormality became painful, I called my friends in the VIP ward. Although they tried not to laugh, it was impossible because I joined right in.

Assisting me into a nearby wheelchair, they took me to the ER. Throughout my embarrassing jaunt to the emergency department, everyone on staff popped over to gawk at the nurse who stuck a needle in her stomach. So much for hiding my humiliation. Receiving care was difficult because, once again, laughter permeated the ER as news of my predicament spread to other departments faster than a forest fire.

After being off work for six weeks because of sharp pain and abdominal distention with no improvement, I consulted an abdominal surgeon who diagnosed my inferior epigastric artery as lacerated. (Arterial bleeding is fast and furious, which explained my left-sided swiftly expanding abdomen.) I couldn't return to work for three months. Are we sensing a theme in my nursing career? However, I learned a vital lesson—be careful when playing with sharp objects.

***

All nurses know their profession involves patients dealing with life-and-death situations. Fear is prevalent, and nurses wear many hats to advocate their needs. We cater to the psychological challenges by listening to their complaints to educate and reassure them. The nurse becomes the patient's last line of defense in the complicated world of medicine. Employing common sense and questioning recommendations that contradict normal effective treatment or supplanting a doctor's lack of assigning appropriate orders are what I call the nurse's version of Stand Your Ground. A principle that served me well as I worked as a charge nurse in the Clinic's VIP Ward—two examples follow.

The first instance involved an intern who deemed writing orders beneath him—after all, he was the doctor, and we were just lowly nurses. He was assigned a patient with a Stage IV decubitus ulcer (the most severe type of bedsore that can extend down to the bone). Sitting at the nurses' station, he spent less than a minute charting orders. When he rose and started to leave, I quickly grabbed the chart. As expected, he neglected to write orders for her relief.

I ran after him. "Excuse me, Dr. Smith, but you didn't write any orders for this patient's painful ulcers."

"Just write whatever you want and sign my name."

"It's your job to provide orders for proper care."

"No, that's the nurse's job," and he walked away.

I was furious and grabbed him by the scruff of his lab coat, literally dragged him back to the nurse's station, and plopped him into a chair. "No, doctor, that's your job. Do it." I handed him the patient's chart and stood behind him, preventing his escape. I didn't realize everyone was staring at me in amazement, but I didn't budge.

With his head down, he finally admitted he didn't know what to write.

"Nurses can be your best allies. All you have to do is ask." I told him what to write, and the chart now contained explicit instructions for care.

Other nurses, staring open-mouthed, asked, "Did you really just drag him back to the station?" I laughed at my knee-jerk response and nodded. They congratulated me on standing up to the intern, who was known for his rude treatment of nurses and superior attitude.

The second case involved strange orders relayed during the nurse's report from the day shift. The patient had a new type of tracheostomy tube, and we were instructed not to suction the tube under any circumstances. A tracheostomy tube (aka Trach) is life-saving care for a patient with a blocked airway. Since inhaled air to the lungs isn't being filtered by the upper airways, diligent suctioning of the inner removable tube (aka cannula) is essential to clear mucous and secretions.

After report, I immediately checked on my patient, who was experiencing severe difficulty breathing as tears of frustration streamed down her face. I ran to the nurse's station and asked the doctor to examine my patient.

After his exam, he shook his head. "I have no idea why she can't breathe."

"Did you know we were told in report not to suction her trach tube?"

His eyes wide in shock, he returned to the room and removed her inner cannula clogged with secretions. Upon removal, she could instantly breathe and was grateful for the relief. Outside the patient's room, the physician thanked me for the insight to ease her compromised breathing before amending chart orders for routine suctioning. When I re-entered the patient's room to suction her airway, she hugged me and laughed with undisguised pleasure as her respirations normalized. Her laughter was so infectious that I joined in as we celebrated a reprieve from her suffocation debacle.

Early in my career, I learned to question orders if they do not alleviate symptoms or hamper a patient's recovery. Being a champion for your patient should be the nurse's top priority, and the gratitude from those in your care will be the most rewarding aspect of nursing. And, if that care invokes laughter from a positive outcome, it truly is the best medicine—especially for nurses.

**About the Author**

Mary Frances Fisher, a lifelong resident of Cleveland, Ohio, is a Registered Nurse with Multi-State Licensure. Her medical career has been diverse, including Charge Nurse on the VIP ward at the Cleveland Clinic's main campus, Medical Analyst, HEDIS Reviewer at WellCare of Ohio, Medical Claims Approver at Metropolitan Insurance, Traveling Nurse escorting patients around the country, Legal Nurse Consultant in addition to working as a Nurse Paralegal for plaintiff and defense firms.

Her writing career includes two award-winning historical fiction novels based on actual events and stories passed down from her family: *Paradox Forged in Blood* is a historical murder mystery, and *Growing Up O'Malley* covers a century of her family history with heart, humor, and historical events. Ms. Fisher is working on her third novel, *When I Grow Up: A Collection of Short Stories*. She has also written a screenplay based on one of her short stories, "Mercy's Legacy".

maryfrancesfisher.com

franfisher1339@gmail.com

# Chapter 13

## Reduce Anxiety and Heal Faster with a Surgery Coach

Chris Duffy Wentzel

My life was turned upside down when, at fifty-two, I received a cancer diagnosis. With my career on the upswing, I didn't have time for cancer! At first, my goal was to get the surgery over with as fast as possible and get back to my life!

Sound familiar?

Yet, something didn't feel right for me. A gnawing feeling in the pit of my stomach told me there was something else happening. On my drive home from the surgical consult, I got to the source of my discomfort. I'm adopted, and since the age of 18, trying, I have been searching for my birth mother. I was mostly interested in my genetic history as I was marrying someone with Cystic Fibrosis in the family. Since my adoption was a closed adoption through Catholic Charities, my records in New Jersey were SEALED, which seemed totally unfair. "Shouldn't the birth mothers at least provide medical updates?" I innocently asked one of the social workers. Her annoyed response was: "We're not a detective agency."

The reality that I was only fifty-two and facing life-changing surgery was crippling. Despite my repeated attempts with the adoption agency to get my medical history so I could find out if cancer was in my family tree, I had to make a decision. I set the surgery date. A good friend gave me Peggy

Huddleston's book "Prepare for Surgery, Heal Faster," as the surgeon convinced me that surgery was the only recourse.

Riveted by Peggy Huddleston's true patient healing stories supported by clinical data, I dog-eared and underlined Peggy's book.

I also read a book about the connection between diseases and the chakras, or energy centers in the body. I froze when I read this passage: Diseases of the 2nd chakra (the reproductive area) had an emotional connection to unresolved sadness, loss, and grief.

It knocked me over as I began to connect with the emotional trauma of being abandoned at birth and never meeting my birth mother. This awareness aligned with Peggy's work, and I found a medical practitioner who also worked with emotional trauma using sound healing. I began to slowly release the emotions I had stored in my body. This work was critical to my healing journey as I eventually found my birth family, and after years of follow-up, my cancer disappeared without the hysterectomy.

It is now my passion to share my personal experience of reducing anxiety, using fewer pain medications, and recovering faster with anyone who is open to mind-body healing techniques. Leveraging the clinical work and mind-body techniques by Harvard Researcher Peggy Huddleston, I offer a Prepare for Surgery, Heal Faster workshop. The 90-minute session focuses on visualization and guided meditation techniques that bring the parasympathetic nervous system online. This reduces the stress response and strengthens the immune system, which promotes healing.

**Physically Prepare**

For those who want to prepare physically for surgery, the first step is to visit www.healfaster.com, Peggy Huddleston's website. The site contains a very helpful radio interview Peggy gave to NPR explaining the clinical data and how many medical centers worldwide have adopted her techniques for all types of surgeries. In addition, a mindfulness-guided visualization recording can be listened to at least once daily. The ideal time to begin preparation is two weeks or more before the surgery date.

I highly suggest finding a Prepare for Surgery coach, as the workshop is customized to each person's needs. It's also important to involve your support team in the Prepare for Surgery process. It's a great idea to suggest that they read the book or attend the workshop with the patient to ensure everyone is aligned along the recovery journey. Visualizing the various steps of recovery is crucial, and it's also important to consider whether the individual's support community is aligned with any lifestyle changes they wish to make.

The most important element is seeing and FEELING a positive outcome. I've worked with individuals who had doubts about the power of the process. Yet even being skeptical, they still used 25-50% less pain meds and recovered faster than their surgeon thought possible.

From my experience, this process has no distinction between body, mind, and spirit. It's all integrated, as scientists have proved the interconnection between the body, mind, and spirit in very specific ways. We know clinically that by reducing stress and anxiety, genes respond differently. People who may have a genetic cancer risk never get cancer as the mechanisms that turn on the genes are not activated. For more information, see Bruce Lipton's book The Biology of Hope or Dr. Joe Dispenza's body of work.

**Spiritually Prepare**

BELIEVE that all things are possible. We are somewhat brainwashed, believing and accepting that a stage 1 cancer diagnosis will progress to stage 4, etc.

What if you held the belief and really felt and visualized full recovery in your soul? That it's possible for the disease to regress and disappear. If the disease came, why can't it leave?

Can we take a detached view of any illness and actually explore what it might be trying to tell us? Can we quiet our minds, ask difficult questions, and truly listen to the answer?

For me, I chose to face the truth that my life was totally out of balance. Yes, I really LOVED my career. At the same time, I was running on fumes and was living in chronic stress. My cancer diagnosis was like hitting a giant PAUSE button on my life. I think part of my complete healing was recognizing the connection between my mind, body, and spirit.

**Maintain a Positive Mindset**

Maintaining a healthy and positive mindset is essential. In addition to personal habits and changes that an individual may make, there is also the realization that there may be people in one's life who are not contributing positively to their lives. Everyone has had experiences where being with certain people makes them feel validated and energized. Then, some people may feel like energy vampires. They suck the life out of us with their negativity. Love and appreciation are the two emotions that help identify and maintain that state. Before going to bed, making a list of all the things we appreciate is a wonderful way to reset. As we wake up in the morning, we acknowledge that we're alive and it's a new day. Being intentional about staying in a high vibration can set a positive tone for the day. It can be as simple as smiling at strangers or engaging store personnel in ways that let them know we appreciate them. Imagine how quickly our world would shift if we started the day with the intention of treating people with respect and kindness.

Meditation and quieting the mind are very helpful in promoting healing. There are many apps that people can use, such as CALM, which offer meditations and music designed with specific frequencies to calm the nervous system. BE HERE NOW, and living in the present moment is a process to explore and imbibe. Eckhart Tolle's work is an excellent, accessible resource. He offers many free YouTube where he shares explicit techniques to cope with grief, anger, negative self-talk, etc. His books, New Earth and the Power of Now, contain practical suggestions and inspirational stories. So much of our time is spent beating ourselves up for past mistakes or worrying about the future, which creates stress and anxiety and helps create the very thing we're trying to avoid. The connection between stress and anxiety on our immune systems is well documented.

The simplest process for returning to the NOW moment is being aware of our breath. Focusing on and observing it can bring us out of the past or future and into the Now, where our power to create what we want to create is possible.

**Communicate With Your Healthcare Team**

Part of the Prepare for Surgery workshop is to review five healing statements that the patient asks the anesthesiologist or nurse in the operating room to repeat as the patient goes under, then midway through the surgery, and as the patient regains consciousness. When a person is under, they are susceptible to the power of suggestion, and healing and recovery begin with these statements. Sometimes, patients ask me if the anesthesiologist or nurse has to abide by your request. The answer is YES. There is a Patient Bill of Rights, and the healing statements fall under their rights. In the thousands of patients that have been helped with this program, there are NO examples of a medical professional refusing a patient's request.

Clinical data shows that using a surgery coach will reduce pain medications by 25-50% and speed up recovery. I have worked with patients getting hip/knee replacements, and they were ready for physical therapy sooner and exceeded their therapist's timeline of recovery by as much as three weeks.

The services of a surgery coach can benefit anyone undergoing a surgical procedure. Throughout my career as a coach, I have had the privilege of being involved in many individuals' transformative healing experiences. Each story is unique, personal, and inspirational as individuals discover their unique path back to wholeness.

**About the Author**

Chris Duffy Wentzel is a best-selling author, adoptee, and personal coach through the Neuroleadership Institute who lives in the New England area. Her private practice focuses on living a joy-filled life and helping individuals manage career and life transitions. She is committed to assisting clients in reaching a state of peacefulness and well-being by reducing chronic stress and improving overall health in body, mind, and spirit. After experiencing incredible results "up close and personal," Chris became trained and certified by Peggy Huddleston to offer the Prepare for Surgery, Heal Faster Workshop.™ Chris has years of experience as an immunovirologist and development director in a medical device organization specializing in women's health.

Chris@kachinawoman.com

# CHAPTER 14

# WELLBEING WITH THE AYURVEDIC CLOCK

SWETA SRIVASTAVA VIKRAM

A client recently told me he goes to the gym after work at 7 p.m. By the time he comes home, showers, cooks, and sits down to eat dinner, it's almost 9 p.m.

I asked, "What time do you go to bed?"

He replied, "Between 11 p.m. and midnight." The next day, he woke up around 7 a.m.

On the surface, he checks all the boxes. He works out daily, cooks fresh dinner, buys produce from Whole Foods, showers (personal hygiene is on-point), and gets 7-8 hours of sleep every night. You must be thinking ... what's the problem here?

When I probed further about the quality of his sleep, digestion, energy levels, and mood—because Ayurveda teaches us that there is a strong mind-body connection and daily routines are integral to our well-being—he confessed he was battling constipation, poor sleep quality, low energy, skin eruptions, and a few other emotional issues.

This is where our conversation about the Ayurvedic clock started!

In the modern world, we look at time differently. The biggest chunk of our day is devoted to our jobs or learning (daycare/school/college). Then, we allocate time for sleep, food, chores, workouts, socializing, hobbies, rest, etc.

Ayurveda says that living in tune with nature's cycles is key to good health. It works with the hours of the day to help you better manage your tasks, health, and energy levels. More on that in a moment. The Ayurvedic clock has been around for a while now. But did you know that the circadian rhythm or biological clock is the same as the Ayurvedic clock? Even Western science recognizes its power.

### Why the Ayurvedic Clock Matters

Ayurveda, a 5,000-year-old science of healing and life from India, teaches us we are a microcosm of Mother Nature. The Ayurvedic clock is intuitive. According to it, there is an ideal time for every activity we do during the day. It suggests aligning the time we eat, sleep, move, rest, and work with Mother Nature's clock and honoring the Ayurvedic doshas. Honoring the Ayurvedic clock helps balance hormones, mitigates stress, and enhances health.

For example, because this client eats late at night and barely has two hours between his last meal and bedtime, he hasn't enough hours to digest his dinner. He tosses and turns at night, leaving him tired, groggy, and lethargic in the morning. Our body relaxes, cleans, replenishes, and detoxifies when we sleep. The time of the day when he should turn inward and rest is when this client works out and eats his biggest meal. As a result, his mind-body is at war with the toxins, lack of rest, weird digestion, and erratic schedule. Despite his efforts to live a healthy life, he can't enjoy simple rest, restoration, sleep, good digestion, or a positive mental outlook because the timings of his activities aren't conducive to healthy living.

Have you noticed how, by sundown, flocks of pigeons or murders of crows fly back to their nests? They know it's time to return home and rest for the night. But humans get their second wind and go out to dinner, exercise, or socialize when nature expects us to slow down and turn inward. The result? We go to war with ourselves and the rhythm of nature. This can open doors to diseases.

Ayurveda teaches that the closer our daily rhythms are aligned with nature's rhythm, the closer we are to achieving balance and wellness for our minds and bodies. If we go against nature's natural cycle, we might experience imbalances and deterioration in our health.

**Doshas and Ayurvedic Clock**

The Ayurvedic clock breaks the day into six periods and tells time in 4-hour dosha blocks. What do I mean by this? According to Ayurveda, three psycho forces exist in every biological organism, known as "doshas."These doshas are given the names Kapha, Pitta, and Vata.

All three Ayurvedic doshas are present in every cell and every tissue of every organism, just in varied proportions. A growing body of research has reported patterns of blood chemistry, genetic expression, physiological states, and chronic diseases associated with each dosha type.[1][1]

Our dosha is neither good nor bad. It is simply our characteristic. Just as everyone has a unique fingerprint, each person has a particular pattern of energy—an individual combination of physical, mental, and emotional characteristics—that comprises their own constitution. Several factors determine this dosha or constitution at conception, and it remains the same throughout one's life.

As we move through life, the proportion of the three doshas constantly fluctuates according to our environment, diet, seasons, climate, age, and many other factors. As they move into and out of balance, the doshas can affect our health, energy level, and general mood.

Ayurveda tells us we are made up of the five elements and individual consciousness. These five elements are space, air, fire, water, and earth.

The combination of these elements gives rise to three Ayurvedic doshas: Kapha, Pitta, and Vata.

**The elements that make up the three Ayurvedic doshas:**

Vata—ether(space) and air

Pitta—fire and water

Kapha—wate rand earth

We experience each dosha twice during a 24-hour cycle: two periods for Vata, two time slots for Pitta, and two periods for Kapha. In 24 hours, we cycle through the three doshas of Vata, Pitta, and Kapha. Each dosha becomes active at certain hours/times of the day.

**How Does the Ayurvedic Clock Work?**

Vata time: 2am-6 am and 2 pm – 6 pm

Kapha time: 6 am -10 am and 6 pm – 10 pm

Pitta time: 10 am – 2 pm and 10 pm – 2 am

**Activities for Vata Time**

Vata time is the period for creativity and meditation. The hours between 2 am and 6 am are considered the most sacred for meditation. The dosha itself is characterized as light, airy, and dry.

Ayurveda explains that the cold nature of Vata dosha, which governs the 2 pm-6 pm time of day, causes body temperature to drop mid-afternoon, making us feel tired and dreamy. This is an excellent time to do creative work. During this afternoon cycle of Vata dosha, the properties of air and ether are naturally more playful and lighter.

## Activities for Pitta Time

The hours between 10 am and 2 pm are when we feel the most focused, sharp, and productive. This is when the energy of pitta dosha is the strongest, and it's best to deal with the most challenging tasks. Pitta's inherent qualities influence this time of the day, so mid-day is also when agni , or our digestive fire, is the strongest. Ayurveda recommends eating the largest meal of the day at this time to ensure optimal digestion and assimilation of nutrients.

The Pitta time of night is from 10:00 p.m. to 2:00 a.m., and it is essential to sleep during this time because it is a time of internal cleansing. If you remain awake during this critical time, you miss out on the benefits of this cleansing time of day.

A 2018study [2][2] found that night owls were nearly twice as likely as early risers to have a psychological disorder and 30% more likely to have diabetes. Their risk for respiratory disease was 23% higher and 22% higher for gastrointestinal disease.

## Activities for Kapha Time

Ever feel lethargic and sluggish if you sleep in late? That's because earth and water elements, which are by their very nature heavy, make up the Kapha dosha. If you wake up between 6 am and 10 am, which is the Kapha time of the morning, these dull and heavy qualities increase within you. Get out of bed in the mornings before you hit Kapha time. This is also the best time to exercise, eat a light breakfast, and gather energy for the day.

The 6 -10 p.m. time frame is good for slowing down and turning inward. Use Kapha's heaviness and dull qualities to be in bed by 10 p.m. so you can fall into a deep sleep. Relaxing hormones such as serotonin and melatonin decline gradually from 10 p.m. onwards.

**Fun Facts about the Ayurvedic Clock**

Every hour is related to a specific organ(s); therefore, the organ will be at its most powerful energy at its respective times. If instead of sleeping at 11 pm, you are eating a burger while working on a creative deadline and washing it down with a beer or two, what do you think happens to the organ that's supposed to be do cleansing and maintenance work at 11 pm, which is the small intestine and stomach? Also, deep transformation and healing occur between 10 pm and 12 pm. In his 2016 book, The Grain Brain Whole Life Plan, neurologist Dr. David Perlmutter writes that after 10 pm, the body metabolizes many waste products, and from 11 pm to 2 am, the immune system recharges itself.

**Parting Words...**

Ayurveda teaches are a miniature version of nature. Understanding the Ayurvedic clock allows us to honor the natural rhythms of the day and harness the energies that prevail during different times. So, if we align our schedule—when we sleep, eat, move, rest, socialize, and wind down—according to the Ayurvedic clock, we honor Mother Nature and the Ayurvedic doshas. This can enhance our sleep, digestion, energy levels, moods, productivity, creativity, quality of relationships, and overall sense of being.

> "Ayurveda is the science of life that teaches us how to live in harmony with nature and the world around us."
> ~ Dr. Robert Svoboda

## About the Author

Sweta Srivastava Vikram is an international speaker, a best-selling author of 14 books, and a certified Grief Coach. and a Doctor of Ayurveda (AD) committed to helping people thrive on their own terms. Her latest and 14th book is *The Loss That Binds Us: 108 Tips on Coping with Grief and Loss* (Loving Healing Press). She has appeared on NBC, NPR, NYT, Ayurveda documentaries, and several other media outlets, raising awareness of Ayurveda, mindfulness, and holistic healing.

swetavikram.com

## Resources

1. https://www.ncbi.nlm.nih.gov/pmc/articles/PMC4719489/

2. https://www.nytimes.com/2018/04/12/well/mind/morning-people-may-live-longer-than-night-owls.html

# Chapter 15

## Direct Primary Care: It's About "Health" Care, Not "Sick" Care

Arlene McCain, MD

The insurance-driven model of conventional healthcare creates an illusion about family medicine: that a once-a-year physical, a twice-yearly medical checkup, and the occasional sick visit are sufficient to promote and support an individual's health and well-being over their lifetime.

If you seldom visit your family doctor, it doesn't necessarily mean you're healthy; it might just mean you're rarely physically sick or emotionally distressed.

The World Health Organization (WHO) defines health as "a state of complete physical, mental, and social well-being, and not just the absence of disease or infirmity."[1] Let's break down this definition of health into two parts.

**Related to Disease:**

The top two leading causes of death in the U.S. are heart disease and cancer. The age-adjusted death rate from heart disease has increased in the past two years, which was the first increase in many years.[2] Plus, 2024 is the first year the US is expected to have more than 2 million new cases of cancer.[3] Although the United States spends more on healthcare than other high-income countries ($4.5 trillion in 2022[4]), it has some of the worst health outcomes: the lowest life expectancy at birth, the highest death rates for treatable or avoidable conditions, and the highest infant and maternal mortality rates. It also has the highest rate of people with multiple chronic conditions and an obesity rate that's almost double the OECD (Organisation for Economic Co-operation and Development) average.[5]

**Related to Wellbeing:**

According to the WHO,

"Well-being is a positive state experienced by individuals and societies. Like health, it is a daily life resource determined by social, economic, and environmental conditions. Well-being encompasses quality of life and the ability of people and societies to contribute to the world with a sense of meaning and purpose. Focusing on well-being supports tracking the equitable distribution of resources, overall thriving, and sustainability. A society's well-being can be determined by the extent to which it is resilient, builds capacity for action, and is prepared to transcend challenges.[6]"

As a "positive" state, we can posit that a sense of joy is foundational to well-being. Are we happy? Not particularly. According to the January 2024 Gallup Mood of the Nation poll, less than half of Americans are "very satisfied" with their lives. Rates of diagnosis and treatment of depression are the highest recorded by Gallup since it began measuring depression using the current form of data collection in 2015.[7] Additionally, the results of the 2024 American Psychiatric Association's annual mental health poll show that U.S. adults are feeling increasingly anxious.[8] In short, even though the US spends twice the amount per person on health compared to other nations to be healthy and happy,[9] U.S. citizens are increasingly ill, depressed, and anxious.

Let's follow the money. Where does all the money go if it's not helping patients? The top 3 expenditures for excess spending go to administrative costs of insurance, administrative costs of providers, and prescription drugs. U.S. prescription drug prices are two to three times those in other OECD countries. U.S. prices are much higher for branded drugs, which account for approximately 80 percent of prescription drug expenditures in the U.S.[10] In short, the conventional U.S. healthcare system is full of bureaucracy and expensive drugs.

What's the alternative? Less bureaucracy and less need for prescription drugs. How do we do that? A robust primary care system. And, beyond that, increased growth of direct primary care practices.

I'm going to address this solution in two parts. First, I will refer to the long-standing recognition of the value of primary care. Second, I will offer my experience regarding the value of direct primary care as a healthcare delivery model.

The strength of family medicine and of a robust primary care system (which includes pediatricians, internists, and ob-gyns) is found in the 4 C's it offers: continuous (long-term), competent (able to diagnose & treat illness and promote health & wellness), cost-effective (prevent illness and treat early to reduce specialist needs or hospitalizations), and convenient (have access to their physician within a reasonable amount of time).[11]

According to the AAFP, family medicine is "the medical specialty which provides continuing, comprehensive health care for the individual and family. It is a specialty in breadth that integrates the biological, clinical, and behavioral sciences.[12]" Family medicine, then, is a unique branch of medicine because it focuses on whole health care: body (biological)-mind (clinical)-spirit/heart (behavioral/relational).

Thus, the once-a-year physical and twice-a-year medical checks are the biological and clinical aspects of family medicine. The relational dynamic of family medicine–the superpower of family medicine–has been replaced with a to-do list for primary care physicians, which takes 26.7 hours a day to complete.[13] On a good day, doctor visits are scheduled for 30 minutes, although you may be waiting for 30 minutes before seeing them and actually only interact with the doctor for 15 of the 30 minutes of your appointment. Family medicine, once talk-driven, is now task-driven.

The behavioral (i.e., relational) part of family medicine is rarely fully addressed to the point where true health and well-being can occur. Have you gone to the doctor for a physical, mentioned being tired, gotten normal labs, and then been advised, almost as an afterthought, to sleep more, exercise more, eat healthier, and follow up next year?

Rather than delving into a person's behaviors—which often result from a skewed relationship with themselves, others, and their larger community—and supporting them through the stages of change until they can sustain healthy lifestyle choices, patients are essentially advised to figure it out themselves.

Am I biased about the benefits of primary care because I'm a family physician? Here's what the U.S. Department of Health and Human Services, whose tagline is "enhancing the health and well-being of all Americans," has stated:

"It is well documented that health systems with a robust primary care base provide better access to health services and have improved health outcomes, lower mortality, and more equity. Strong primary care can also result in significant cost savings... Robust primary care is essential for addressing behavioral health.[14]"

The behavioral health aspect of primary care, which empowers patients to advocate for themselves and allows physicians to support patients in modifying unhealthy behaviors to promote healthy ones, has been squeezed out of the normal primary care interaction to the point that it's now its own medical specialty - lifestyle medicine!

And what is said about lifestyle medicine?

- "Multiple studies have shown that lifestyle interventions can effectively prevent and treat various chronic diseases.[15]" This includes the top two causes of death in the U.S. (heart disease and cancer), thus improving physical health.

- "Similarly, stress reduction techniques such as meditation and yoga have been found to improve mental health outcomes and reduce the risk of developing depression and anxiety,[15]" thus leading to happier people.

- "In addition to the health benefits, lifestyle medicine can also be cost-effective by reducing the need for expensive medical interventions [15]," which reduces healthcare spending.

- "Furthermore, lifestyle interventions are often low-cost or even free, making them accessible to a wide range of people [15]," which saves money.

According to the WHO, lifestyle interventions prevent 80% of heart disease, stroke, and type 2 diabetes, as well as 40% of cancer diagnoses. However, truly sustainable lifestyle interventions necessitate a relationship where physicians know their patients, patients feel safe to be vulnerable with their physicians, and there are multiple opportunities for connection and accountability. After all, how often is it that we start to make lifestyle changes that last only for two weeks and then give up until next year's New Year's resolutions are made? How often do we get discouraged by our imperfections and give up? With direct primary care (DPC), the relationship is such that it's possible to try and try again, confident that your physician is supporting you, cheering you on, and holding you accountable.

The DPC model of care is an outgrowth of a focus on reduced administrative burdens and increased time with patients. DPC has seen significant growth recently, with memberships increasing by 241% from 2017 to 2021.[16] As of July 2023, there were more than 2,000 DPC practices in the United States, spread across 48 states.[17]

Direct primary care is a physician-led movement that is both an alternative payment and alternative care model. How so?

Alternative payment: This is the "direct" part of DPC. Patients pay physicians a monthly membership fee (so you'll also hear DPC coined as "membership medicine"). This allows the physician to maintain a significantly smaller patient panel (instead of 2500+ patients, they care for fewer than 600 patients) and smaller office staff, leading to longer in-person appointments (30-60 minutes) and multiple opportunities to conveniently access physicians via phone, text, and even home visits. Removing insurance specifically from the patient-physician relationship significantly reduces administrative costs. Patients still use insurance for needs outside the physician-patient relationship–including labs, imaging, medications, and specialist care. Insurance does not cover membership fees, nor can HSAs be used. However, some FSA plans may be used to cover membership fees.

Alternative care: This is the return of primary care to its roots. Beyond the focus on "sick" care (treating acute illness, managing chronic conditions) and task-driven protocols (checking off the routine health maintenance tasks to be done like labs, mammograms, colonoscopies, etc.), it re-incorporates the "health" care aspect by allowing time for shared decision-making.

In this model of care, your physician addresses all the medical conditions they usually would in an office visit, with additional opportunities to address lifestyle and behavioral changes. There are opportunities to meet you where you are and to meet with you according to your needs.

There's a saying about DPC practices, "once you've seen one DPC practice, you've seen one DPC practice." Each practice is operated by a healthcare provider that can offer primary care services. However, depending on that person's unique interests, what a DPC practice offers outside primary care can be very different. For example, I may see a patient once a year, once a month, once a week, or once a day, depending on their physical, emotional, mental, or spiritual needs at a given time. I may meet them via telehealth, in the office, at their home, in a coffee shop, or on a walking trail. And during those meetings, we can address questions like:

- "What are your health goals currently?" When I see your diabetes is uncontrolled, and you tell me you recently lost your wife and are eating casseroles your neighbors are bringing you, then your goal isn't to eat better. Your goal is to navigate grief.

- "What are your barriers to change?" Suppose you're not drinking enough water, but you're a perimenopausal teacher with urinary incontinence when you sneeze or laugh. You can't go to the bathroom whenever you have the urge. In that case, the focus isn't on drinking more water now but perhaps addressing pelvic floor dysfunction during the summer break.

- "What are the ways in which you self-sabotage?" You know a healthy lifestyle includes nourishing foods, regular activity, restful sleep, and stress management. But why do you overgive to others, care constantly for others, and please others, yet deplete yourself, reject yourself, and make yourself miserable?

My experience with DPC is that it promotes more than good medicine. It allows for health and healing for both patients and physicians. That's the gift I have given and received through DPC. Other physicians in other DPC practices offer their unique talents to contribute to the health of patients and the healthcare system. Through the diversity of DPC practices, we discover opportunities for patients from a wide diversity of patients to find physicians who can help them on their personal healthcare journeys towards thriving lives.

A critique of DPC is that such practices, with their smaller patient panels, contribute to physician access issues during a growing physician shortage. I would respond that, in a healthcare system where physician burnout (physicians are retiring early, seeking non-clinical jobs, or paying more attention to a computer than the patient in front of them) and patient distrust are rampant, DPC is an alternative that allows for medical practice to be sustainable, compassionate, and relational. It is a beckoning light for medical students who would not otherwise consider primary care. It allows for physician autonomy, creativity, and flexibility. It allows patients to speak up for themselves, learn healthy boundaries, and re-establish trust in the healthcare system.

My practice includes integrative well-being. The goals are love and liberation; the task is to be gentle with ourselves while walking your health journey together. I intentionally create space for personal growth, health prevention, chronic disease management, and acute care. There's room for health and healing at multiple levels—physically, mentally, emotionally, spiritually, and relationally. There's an exploration of various forms of love: self-love, family love, community love, love for the world, and universal love.

Direct primary care deserves praise for protecting the heart of medicine by preserving the relationships between patients and physicians committed to healthcare.

**About the Author**

Arlene McCain, MD, is a board-certified family physician committed to partnering with individuals as they discern personal motivations for healthy change and passionately support their inspired progress toward a thriving life. Through integrative health coaching, she honors individuals as the ultimate experts in their healing journeys. By integrating family medicine and health coaching, she creates a safe and sacred space in which health and healing can occur.

Dr. McCain earned a Bachelor of Science in Biology and a minor in Theology from Georgetown University. She graduated from Eastern Virginia Medical School and served as chief resident at EVMS-Portsmouth Family Medicine. She later earned a graduate certification in Integrative Health and Wellbeing Coaching through the Center for Spirituality &

Healing at the University of Minnesota. She became one of the first nationally board-certified health and wellness coaches (NBC-HWC) in the nation.

Above all, she is a heart-centered leader whose core value offer is Fierce High Service.

mccainwhc.com

**Resources**

https://www.who.int/about/governance/constitution

https://newsroom.heart.org/news/more-than-half-of-u-s-adults-dont-know-heart-disease-is-leading-cause-of-death-despite-100-year-reign

https://www.cancer.org/research/acs-research-news/facts-and-figures-2024.html

https://www.cms.gov/data-research/statistics-trends-and-reports/national-health-expenditure-data/historical

https://www.cnn.com/2023/01/31/health/us-health-care-spending-global-perspective/index.html

https://www.who.int/activities/promoting-well-being

https://news.gallup.com/poll/505745/depression-rates-reach-new-highs.aspx

https://www.psychiatry.org/news-room/news-releases/annual-poll-adults-express-increasing-anxiousness

https://www.pgpf.org/blog/2023/07/how-does-the-us-healthcare-system-compare-to-other-countries

https://www.commonwealthfund.org/publications/issue-briefs/2023/oct/high-us-health-care-spending-where-is-it-all-going#:~:text=Key%20Findings%20and%20Conclusion:%20More,Introduction

https://teamcaremedicine.com/robust-primary-care/

https://www.aafp.org/about/policies/all/family-medicine-definition.html

https://news.uchicago.edu/story/primary-care-doctors-would-need-more-24-hours-day-provide-recommended-care#:~:text=For%20an%20average%20number%20of,available%20in%20any%20given%20day.

https://www.hhs.gov/blog/2023/11/07/us-department-health-and-human-services-taking-action-strengthen-primary-care.html

SadiqIZ. Lifestyle medicine as a modality for prevention and management of chronicdiseases. J Taibah Univ Med Sci. 2023 Apr 15;18(5):1115-1117. doi:10.1016/j.jtumed.2023.04.001. PMID: 37187803; PMCID: PMC10176046.

https://www.medicaleconomics.com/view/high-cost-of-health-care-may-be-boosting-direct-primary-care-membership

https://www.elationhealth.com/resources/blogs/direct-primary-care-mapper-how-many-dpc-practices-are-in-the-us-today

# Chapter 16

# A Journey: Tick-Borne Illnesses and Mast Cell Activation Syndrome

Summer Le'Dawn

Have you ever felt like something was wrong with your body, but at every doctor's visit, you felt more confused than before? That was my reality for over a decade as I embarked on a journey to unravel the mystery of my debilitating symptoms. What started as unexplained throat swelling, pain, and nausea turned into a long and difficult quest for a proper diagnosis and effective treatment.

Initially, my symptoms were dismissed as manifestations of anxiety and simple allergies. Medications prescribed to me only seemed to exacerbate my condition, leading to even more distressing reactions. It wasn't until multiple rounds of blood work and tests were conducted that I was finally diagnosed with Rocky Mountain Spotted Fever, Alpha-gal Syndrome, and Lyme, which are all tick-borne illnesses. However, this discovery was just the beginning of a series of baffling encounters with specialists and skeptics who questioned the legitimacy of my illnesses.

"Are you sure this isn't all in your head?"

These words struck a chord deep within me, igniting my determination to seek the truth about my health. However, this was just the tip of the iceberg. My journey led me to the discovery of an immune condition known as Mast Cell Activation Syndrome, a diagnosis not widely known among the medical community at the time. It was only through my own extensive research and the support of fellow patients in similar situations that I was able to uncover the true nature of my illness (MCAS.)

Mast cells are crucial to the body's immune system, acting as vigilant defenders against foreign substances. Positioned strategically throughout the body, from the skin into various internal organs, mast cells can release over 200 chemical mediators when activated, resulting in multiple symptoms. Tick-borne diseases can trigger mast cells, causing them to combat the pathogens by releasing these chemical mediators. The body's defense mechanism can misidentify harmless substance as threats after enduring prolonged exposure to untreated tick-borne illnesses, leading to ongoing battles with allergic reactions to everyday elements such as foods, medications, chemicals, and environmental factors. This underscores the significant impact of tick-borne diseases on the body's immune response, highlighting the importance of timely detection and treatment.

Despite the doctor's grim prognosis that I wouldn't make it much longer and years of surviving on a limited diet while confined to a wheelchair because of malnutrition stemming from (MCAS), I clung to hope more than ever before. Through unwavering perseverance and the support of like-minded individuals, I not only gained clarity about my condition but also discovered a natural treatment that brought about a dramatic turnaround in my health.

This experience has taught me the invaluable lesson of the importance of self-advocacy and empowerment in the healthcare journey. For patients and healthcare professionals alike, it is vital to remain open-minded and persistent when faced with unexplained symptoms and elusive diagnoses.

Knowledge and understanding are crucial to providing accurate diagnoses and proper treatment in healthcare. However, a shocking lack of awareness among healthcare professionals about mast cell activation syndrome and tick-borne diseases has led to significant suffering for many patients. This lack of education has resulted in misdiagnoses, mistreatment, and neglect, leaving many patients feeling abandoned by the very system designed to help them.

I've spoken with various members of the medical community from all across the country and in my home state of Alabama, including specialists, family practitioners, and nurses. I was taken aback to find that 90% of them had little to no knowledge of mast cell activation syndrome. Additionally, most of these healthcare professionals were poorly educated on tick-borne diseases and how to diagnose and properly treat them. This has led to numerous instances of patients being dismissed and disbelieved, facing the heartbreaking reality of being labeled as "crazy" and told that their symptoms are "all in their head."

Throughout my journey, I have met so many amazing patients, but the stories I've encountered are deeply troubling. Patients with genuine medical conditions have been subjected to dismissive and derogatory attitudes from healthcare providers. Many have been wrongfully admitted to psychiatric facilities against their will solely because their physicians lacked the understanding to recognize and address their physical ailments.

At the beginning of my battle, I was misdiagnosed with anxiety when I presented symptoms that clearly indicated a serious medical issue. My allergist admitted to being unable to provide an answer because of his lack of knowledge, and a surgeon refused to perform a necessary surgery, claiming that my conditions were "in my head" because he had never heard of them. The CDC sent me to an infectious disease specialist at the state's leading teaching medical school, and the I.D. doctor laughed in my face and said he didn't care what the test results said and that we do not have tick-borne diseases in our state and then he proceeded to leave the room.

The consequences of this pervasive ignorance in the medical community are severe. Countless patients have endured unnecessary suffering, harassment, and a worsening of their conditions due to the absence of appropriate treatment. In some tragic cases, patients have developed PTSD as a result of the trauma and neglect they experienced at the hands of uninformed healthcare professionals, and even worse, many patients have lost their lives.

The impact is not limited to the patients alone. Family members, such as spouses, have also been deeply affected by the lack of understanding within the healthcare system. The stress and anguish of witnessing a loved one suffer due to inadequate medical care can cause secondary trauma, resulting in signs of PTSD.

This alarming reality underscores the urgent need for improved education and awareness among healthcare professionals worldwide. Patients should not have to endure additional suffering and trauma simply because their doctors are ill-equipped to recognize and address their medical conditions.

The medical community must prioritize ongoing education and training to stay informed about all potential medical conditions and treat patients with the respect, dignity, and care they deserve. Only with increased knowledge and understanding can healthcare professionals fulfill their crucial role of providing accurate diagnoses and effective treatment for all patients, regardless of the complexity of their conditions.

To those grappling with the uncertainties of chronic illness, I extend a message of hope and solidarity. Embrace the power of knowledge, remain steadfast in your pursuit of answers, and never underestimate the impact of unwavering determination. Remember, looking for a healthcare provider knowledgeable in functional and naturopathic medicine is essential. This holistic approach to healthcare can provide a more comprehensive understanding of your health and well-being, addressing both the symptoms and the underlying causes of your health issues.

It's important to remember that, as a patient, you are in charge of your health. Your healthcare provider works for you, not the other way around. Having someone by your side who can advocate for you and ensure that you receive the care and attention you deserve is vital. If you ever feel ignored, bullied, or harassed by your doctor or their staff, it's time to seek a new healthcare provider who will treat you with the respect and compassion you deserve.

Furthermore, a good healthcare provider genuinely cares for their patients. They should spend time with you, actively listen to your concerns, and show compassion for your health struggles. It's important to find a provider who focuses on finding the root cause of your health issues rather than simply prescribing medications as a quick fix that only masks the problem. A healthcare provider who pushes pills without exploring alternative treatments and lifestyle changes may not have your best interests at heart.

Moreover, it is of the utmost importance to be aware of lesser-known health conditions such as mast cell activation syndrome and tick-borne diseases. Unfortunately, few healthcare providers are well-versed in these areas, leaving patients with limited options for specialized care. It's essential for the medical community to become more educated about these conditions to better serve patients in need.

You should be discerning when choosing a healthcare provider. While some may prioritize financial gain over patient care, others are genuinely committed to helping individuals achieve better health. Patients and healthcare professionals alike should be vigilant in discerning between providers who are solely focused on profit and those who are dedicated to improving the well-being of their patients.

In conclusion, selecting the right healthcare provider is instrumental in managing your health effectively. By seeking providers who are knowledgeable, compassionate, and committed to addressing the root causes of health issues, patients can receive the quality care they deserve. Likewise, healthcare professionals should strive to embody these qualities to provide the best possible care for their patients. Advocating for a healthcare system that prioritizes patient well-being above all else is crucial.

As a medical patient, it's easy to feel isolated and overwhelmed. The constant battle with illness can make us doubt our own bodies and feel like we're losing our minds. We do need to acknowledge the emotional and mental toll that illness can take. It's okay to feel frustrated, angry, or even hopeless at times. These emotions are a natural response to the challenges you're facing. But amidst the struggle, please remember that your life truly matters. You are not defined by your illness but rather by the unique qualities that make you who you are. Your illness may be a part of your life, but it does not diminish your worth or purpose.

Trusting your body can be daunting, especially when it seems to work against you. Chronic pain, discomfort, and uncertainty can erode your confidence in your body's ability to heal and persevere. While medical guidance is essential, trusting your instincts and advocating for your needs is equally important. You know your body better than anyone else, and your intuition can provide valuable insights into your health.

Finally, I highly recommend finding a supportive community, as it can make a world of difference. Connecting with others who are going through similar experiences can provide comfort, validation, and helpful resources. Whether in-person support groups, online forums, or social media communities, surrounding yourself with understanding individuals can help you feel less isolated and more empowered. Your experiences, challenges, and triumphs have the potential to resonate with and support others who are traveling a similar path. Embracing and sharing your story with empathy and authenticity can create meaningful connections and build a supportive network of individuals who understand and celebrate your resilience. You are resilient, valuable, and worthy of compassion and support.

## About the Author

Summer Le'Dawn is a passionate outdoor enthusiast hailing from Alabama whose life took an unexpected turn when she contracted Rocky Mountain Spotted Fever, Lyme disease, and Alpha-Gal Syndrome from a single tick bite. This unfortunate encounter led to a harrowing journey with Mast Cell Activation Syndrome, a condition that nearly claimed her life in early 2018. Rather than succumbing to adversity, she transformed her experiences into a mission. As the founder of TickedOffMastCells.org, she strives to illuminate the often-overlooked dangers of tick-borne illnesses. Summer's book, *Canary in a Bubble*, serves as a clarion call, shedding light on the intricate symptoms and challenges of these diseases.

Summer's website provides essential resources on Mast Cell Activation Syndrome and tick-borne disease, empowering others with knowledge and support. She is dedicated to educating both the medical community and the public to foster understanding and prevention. Join her in this vital cause as we unravel the complexities of tick-borne diseases and advocate for those affected.

TickedOffMastCells.org

CanaryinaBubble@gmail.com

# Chapter 17

# How Childhood Trauma Surfaces and What To Do About It

Leslie Ferguson, MFA

The undertow took me when I was six. It was the first time I believed I was going to die. But a surfer on the beach rescued me and my family. He didn't know us, yet he responded to an emergency like any hero would, and instead of ending up in a body bag, I made it to our apartment with heavy lungs, where I emptied clumps of sand from the crotch of my swimsuit.

The second time I believed I was going to die, I woke up to my mom strangling me so hard my jugular pulsed like a time bomb ticking away the minutes of my life.

Many of us might say we've had brushes with death. But how many of us have felt such terror at the hands of a parent? The difference matters. A child's sense of safety at home influences their later success and wellness.

Adverse Childhood Experiences (ACE) is a term coined by the Centers for Disease Control and Kaiser Permanente, a healthcare organization in California that conducted a study in 1995 that "referred to three specific kinds of adversity children faced in the home environment—various forms of physical and emotional abuse, neglect, and household dysfunction." The study showed adverse childhood experiences are common, with nearly half of all subjects reporting one and 25% of respondents reporting two (out of a ten). The study also revealed that persons who had experienced four or more categories of childhood exposure, compared to those who had experienced none, had 4- to 12-fold increased health risks for alcoholism, drug abuse, depression, and suicide attempt; a 2- to 4-fold increase in smoking, poor self-rated health, ≥50 sexual intercourse partners, and sexually transmitted disease; and a 1.4- to 1.6-fold increase in physical inactivity and severe obesity" (Felitti et al. 245).

My ACE score is 8/10.

This means my childhood was horrific enough to cause potential lifelong issues: mental, physical, social, emotional, and financial.

I was one of those at-risk children, a kid who regularly experienced fear and violence in the household, a kid whose parents were divorced, and whose mom was a mentally ill alcoholic who threatened my life daily. My mother did love me, or she would not have tried to kill me (an act she believed would save me from a worse fate), right? Now that I know more about schizophrenia, her disease, it is easier to forgive her for her trespasses against me—easier to forgive her for my childhood impoverishment, neglect, malnourishment, and homelessness.

How did I survive? I think the first answer to this question is literal: I woke up before she could finish the job.

The other answers are more complicated. I survived by luck and by a confluence of resiliency factors that played an important role in not only my survival but also my ability to thrive despite such a precarious early upbringing.

One resiliency factor came when I was eleven. I was removed from my mother's custody but still at risk, suffering in an abusive and neglectful foster home. Then, I was placed in the right sixth-grade classroom, under the education of the right teacher, at just the right time.

My grandparents helped me build resiliency, too. When I was eight, my brother and I lived with them, and their influence on my life was not small. They took custody of us while my mom was jailed and hospitalized, fed us well, encouraged our efforts in school, and rewarded us for good grades. They gave us a small allowance each week and matched every cent we put in savings, and they protected us from our mom . . . until they no longer could. My mother was a vicious force of nature, and she put my grandparents in harm's way, too, threatening them and returning again and again to kidnap my brother and me. The last time landed her in jail again. She had driven my brother and me to the high desert, where the cops found us. However, nobody knew, save for my brother and me, that she planned to kill us. If the police had not found us, I am sure we would have died.

The ACEs study confirms there is a powerful, persistent correlation between the more ACEs experienced and the greater the chance of poor outcomes later in life, including dramatically increased risk of heart disease, diabetes, obesity, depression, substance abuse, smoking, poor academic achievement, time out of work, and early death" ("What Are Aces?").

What the ACEs study doesn't show is how crucial the role of resiliency is in the lives of those exposed to toxic stress caused by adverse experiences suffered over time. Now we know that if a child is regularly exposed to even a few factors of resiliency in their life, such as a reliable and supportive adult who can help with building core life skills and providing guidance during tough situations, the child has a far greater chance of success and wellness (physically and mentally) later in life.

Physician and award-winning author Gabor Maté, in his book *When the Body Says No: Exploring the Stress-Disease Connection,* acknowledges that the beliefs we inhabit about ourselves from an early age influence how we respond to stress over the years. He says, "[These beliefs] control our behaviors no matter what we may think on the conscious level. They keep us in shut-down defensive modes or allow us to open to growth and to health" (231). When we can open ourselves up to a more positive set of beliefs, we can see that we are lovable and worthy of help and friendship, which can promote healing.

When my teacher and her husband took me in, they kick-started my healing journey. They could have given up on me thousands of times. I was surly, defiant, bold . . . and I was a people-pleasing binge-eater, hiding my past and my worst thoughts and emotions, mostly because I did not understand my own anger. I hated myself for all I had been through. But my teacher and her husband continued to show me love, strength, and perseverance. If they would not give up on me, how could I give up on myself? Their unconditional support allowed me to see that I had value. They put me back together again after all I had learned how to do was fall apart.

But I had to open myself up to their love and support to experience joy and confidence. I had to figure out who I was after being so wounded and caught up in trying to be who I thought everyone else wanted me to be. I had to soften enough to let their support hold me up, and I had to use it for what it was—a pillar, not a panacea. I had to accept a path toward healing and safety.

Not every child will find such a responsible, caring, generous family willing to do the hard work of raising a lost kid. It is true that luck, or fate, is partially what has saved me. My resiliency score is high—it would have to be for me to be here, alive, sharing my truth. After so much went wrong in my childhood, a lot had to go right in the years since I was removed from my mom's custody. I am an All-American athlete and a successful college graduate with two master's degrees, two decades of teaching, and an award-winning memoir under my belt. Nobody else did that for me. Yes, I had resources, support, stability, and safety. But those advantages did not erase my trauma. They equipped me with enough coping skills to heal in small ways over many years.

My high ACE score made me highly susceptible to chronic illness and disease, which might explain the many health concerns I deal with regularly. I didn't inherit my biological mother's schizophrenia. But my traumatized body and mind made perfect breeding grounds for fibromyalgia, migraines, anxiety, hypervigilance, low self-esteem, chronic fatigue, binge eating, depression, joint, and muscle pain, and reproductive and digestive problems.

Chronic Illness and disability activist Kirsten Schultz gives us hope. She acknowledges that "ACEs are mostly preventable" (Schultz). The Center on the Developing Child at Harvard University offers that, "for those who have experienced ACEs, there are a range of responses that can help, including therapeutic sessions with mental health professionals, meditation, physical exercise, spending time in nature, and many others. The ideal approach, however, is to *prevent* the need for these responses by reducing the sources of stress in people's lives." ("What Are Aces?").

Schultz adds that we "must take traumatic experiences in childhood more seriously. Once we do that, we'll be able to understand the link between illness and trauma better—and perhaps prevent health issues for our children in the future" (Schultz).

But trauma cannot be undone, so how can we improve life after trauma?

We need society to play a role in the development of all children by becoming trauma-informed. We need parents and families to become educated about how important it is to love and support kids and to promote the healthiest home environment possible. The responsibility of caring for children is great; families shouldn't have to do it alone. We need teachers, counselors, and coaches who provide stability and encouragement and believe in every child's capacity for greatness. Ultimately, "fostering strong, responsive relationships between children and their caregivers, and helping children and adults build core life skills, can help to buffer a child from the effects of toxic stress" and "prevent and counteract lasting harm" ("What Are Aces?").

For most of my life, my favorite tool was denial. Unfortunately, denial isn't a cure for trauma. In his book, *The Body Keeps the Score: Brain, Mind, and Body in the Healing of Trauma*, Bessel van der Kolk, M.D., says, "Erasing awareness and cultivating denial is often essential to survival, but the price is that you lose track of who you are, of what you are feeling, and of what and whom you can trust" (136). Eventually, I needed to face my damaging childhood so I could access my true self. I could only exist on the surface for so long before my body responded to pent-up anger, fear, numbness, and resentment. The first symptoms of my childhood were headaches, chronic fatigue, unexplained back pain, and restless legs. Doctors couldn't explain any of it because their tests all showed there was nothing wrong with me. None of them considered my childhood—none of them asked.

At some point, *I* had to consider that my childhood was to blame for my body's failures. This was when I started to take responsibility for my trauma by acknowledging it, so I could process it and move out of the past and into the present.

Thankfully, many ways exist to increase mindfulness and body awareness for emotion regulation, stress reduction, and mood and health improvement. Here are some things that have fostered my resiliency and helped me process my childhood:

**Expanding My Inner World**

Acupuncture

Breathing and stretching routines

Cognitive-behavioral therapy

Coloring

EMDR therapy

Jewelry making

Journaling

Listening to music

Massage

Meditation

Painting

Physical therapy

Reading

Striving for a healthy work-life balance

Walking in nature

Writing and publishing a memoir about my trauma and healing journey

Writing poetry

Yoga

**Expanding My Outer World**

Building valuable relationships

Exploring new places

Helping others discover their own healing potential, writing voice, and critical thinking abilities

Interacting with other creative people

Making time for play and laughter

Playing sports and being a part of a team

Spending time with people I can trust and learn from

We can do so much to help ourselves, but it's important to remember that we are not meant to exist alone in this world.

Bessel van der Kolk confirms that "traumatized beings recover in the context of relationships [with others]" and that "the role of those relationships is to provide physical and emotional safety, including safety from feeling shamed, admonished, or judged, and to bolster the courage to tolerate, face, and process the reality of what has happened" (212). Over time, if we have enough people doing right by us, those messages of despair we harbor can begin to fall away, revealing the truth about who we are.

Little by little, with others' help, we can come to see ourselves with love and care. This is one of the greatest indicators of resiliency. Perhaps it is the greatest trick of all, and it happens when nobody is watching. We can barely notice when we shift into wholeness. Many steps add up to a completed journey, and we must not give up even when the road seems long.

I can't go back and redo my childhood. And I wouldn't want to. I am the woman I am because of my trauma—and also because of my resiliency. Logically, I know I am not in imminent danger anymore, even though my body's sympathetic nervous system is still trying to fight off threats and hold up the universe. I remain in a steady state of fight or flight, as do most trauma survivors. This is proof that my body has kept the score. I try to remember to let my body feel what it feels so it doesn't hold all that pain in—because damage needs to breathe in order to heal. While I wish I didn't have to manage so many physical ailments, living in this body reminds me that I am a survivor. I hope it also means I have greater compassion for others and can extend kindness that might aid others on their journey toward safety and healing.

The path may be different for everyone, but I know if we acknowledge our trauma, reduce stress, and ask for guidance and assistance when we need it, we can build more resiliency and hope.

We must be a society of helpers, a world of people who love and protect children, lift each other up, and lead by example. We must never give up on anyone, least of all ourselves.

Now, I am not going to take in an eleven-year-old kid. I'm no saint. But I have learned how to be a better parent to myself. And I have taken in a husband and two rescue cats. Most days, I find I'm able to live in hope and gratitude. And most days, that is enough. And when you get there, you'll see . . . it's quite a beautiful place to be.

**About the Author**

Leslie Ferguson is the author of *When I Was Her Daughter* (Acorn Publishing, 2021) *and* winner of twelve awards, including the Readers' Favorite Gold Medal for Memoir, the Memoir Prize for Books, and the Pencraft Book Award. A Southern California native and former foster youth, she holds an MA in English literature and an MFA in creative writing from Chapman University. Leslie taught high school English for two decades before joining the publishing industry in San Diego in 2019. An active board member of the International Memoir Writers Association, Leslie enjoys participating as a member of the San Diego Writers and Editors Guild, SD/PEN, and the Editorial Freelancers Association. As a memoir expert and writing coach, she is passionate about encouraging others to tell their stories. As an editor and publishing specialist, Leslie spends much of her time helping writers realize their literary dreams. Her work has been published in various literary magazines and anthologies, including *The Ekphrastic Review, Tiny Spoon, Coffin Bell, and Shaking the Tree, Volume 5.* She is currently working on her second book.

LeslieFergusonAuthor.com

LeslieFerguson@LeslieFergusonAuthor.com

**Sources Cited**

Felitti, Vincent J., M.D., FACP, et al. "Relationship of Childhood Abuse and Household Dysfunction to Many of the Leading Causes of Death in Adults: The Adverse Childhood Experiences (ACE) Study." *American Journal of Preventive Medicine,* vol. 14. Issue 4, May 1998, 245–258, https://www.ajpmonline.org/article/S0749-3797(98)00017-8/pdf. 28 August 2024.

Maté, Gabor, M.D. *When the Body Says No: Exploring the Stress-Disease Connection.* John Wiley & Sons, Inc., 2003.

*Schultz, Kirsten.* "Are Childhood Trauma and Chronic Illness Connected?" *Healthline. com,* 18 Sept. 2018, https://www.healthline.com/health/chronic-illness/childhood-trauma-connected-chronic-illness#Whats-next?. 28 Aug. 2024.

Van der Kolk, Bessel, M.D. *The Body Keeps the Score: Brain, Mind, and Body in the Healing of Trauma*. Penguin Books, 2015.

"What Are Aces? And How Do They Relate to Toxic Stress?" *Center on the Developing Child*, Harvard University, 30 Oct. 2020, developingchild.harvard.edu/resources/aces-and-toxic-stress-frequently-asked-questions/#:~:text=These%20three%20principles%E2%80%94reducing%20stress,long%2Dterm%20effects%20of%20ACEs. 28 Aug. 2024.

# Chapter 18

## Living Well with Boundaries

Glen Alex

We often hear people talk about boundaries. Healthy boundaries. So, what exactly is a boundary, and why are they essential to your health and wellness? Boundaries comprise your innate alarm system, which is monitored by your intuition – your inner wisdom. Please focus on the words innate and intuition because you are born with boundaries and intuition; thus, both are ingrained in who you are and are available to you 24 hours a day, seven days a week. No one can separate you from your boundaries, from your inherited armor. As such, your boundaries alert you when you are in danger from another person or a perilous situation.

Even though your boundaries are innate and ever-present, you can disconnect from or ignore them. Issues such as fear, mental and emotional constraints, and abusive or unsatisfying relationships often cause disconnection. Ignoring or dismissing your boundaries is giving your personal power away, allowing someone else to define your reality and dictate your narrative, either of which can lead to anxiety, depression, and poor self-care. One of my goals is to help you reconnect with and respect your innate armor so you can live fully, be healthy, and experience authentic love and joy.

Self-awareness is crucial for healthy boundaries. Identifying your boundaries without knowing where you begin and end as a person and where another person begins and ends is impossible.

Without self-awareness, you confuse your thoughts, feelings, emotions, needs, and responsibilities with those of the other person.

One way to develop better self-awareness is to be present. Attuning to what you think, feel, do, and experience at any given moment connects you with your intuition and clarity. When you are mindful, you're able to discern your Personal Truth. Mindfulness is enhanced through meditation, deep breathing, journaling, and mindful movement like yoga.

**The Signs**

There are many signs of unhealthy boundaries. Unfortunately, too many people ignore the red flags that usually appear in the early stages of relationships. A few common ones are:

1. Intuition – a hunch, knowing without knowing why, unease, hair raised on your skin. These signs from your intuition tell you something is off or not right. Instead of paying attention to the red flag, most people dismiss their intuition, downplay or ignore the warning, and make excuses for the other person's inappropriate behavior.

One client was on a second date when the date bragged about tracking down his boss at home. He was persistent in getting his boss to give him a raise. The client shivered (her intuition) as the date described his stalking. She never saw him again.

2. Oversharing – telling too much about yourself too soon. Healthy relationships take time to develop. Those who overshare want to rush the process or entice the other person to rescue them from financial woes, a negative home life, or the like. Such intentions leave the oversharer vulnerable to physical, mental, emotional, or sexual abuse.

A client shared that he tends to reveal his deeply personal information early on to establish a connection with romantic interests and platonic friends. He explained that by sharing everything about himself upfront, he hoped to bring them closer to him and make them see how much he needed them to make him happy. This client is in therapy to address the depression caused by mistreatment from others.

3. Disapproval – abusive and manipulative people often control with negative criticism of how you dress, speak, and relate to others, chipping away at your self-confidence and esteem; to position themselves as the only viable source of worth in your life.

**More Red Flags**

Here are some additional red flags or warning signs showing when a boundary violation may escalate into a more serious issue, such as emotional or physical abuse. These are a few cornerstones of domestic and intimate partner violence:

1. Threats to beat or leave or commit suicide–coercion and emotional blackmail

2. Blocking the door or path to restrict the movement of another person–control

3. Limiting or discouraging contact with loved ones–isolation

4. Blaming others for their failures and misfortunes, never taking personal responsibility for their choices and consequences–narcissism

Keep in mind that abusive and manipulative people rarely show their controlling aggressiveness right away. Consider being on a first or second date, and your romantic interest slaps or leaves you stranded. That will most likely be the last time you see them. So; they groom, insidiously taking control of you instead. Their aggression remains concealed until you become attached and feel dependent on them. Paying attention to red flags can prevent you from getting in too deep with an abuser.

Above are just a few of the many warning signs. The most effective approach to handling them is to proactively maintain self-awareness and clearly define your limits regarding what you will and won't accept from others. So pay attention when you have a hunch or experience oversharing or disapproval. Then, decide if the red flag is a behavior you can live with. If not, permit yourself to leave that person or situation.

**Communication**

Individuals can learn in therapy to affirm and communicate their boundaries clearly, respectfully, and with conviction. And those who support that individual's well-being will adjust. Here are a few strategies to communicate boundaries effectively and assertively, especially when your boundaries are challenged or ignored.

First, communicating boundaries effectively and assertively requires clarity about the boundary, which ties to self-awareness. Many people are too vague about their boundaries. For example, clients say they want to be respected. Respect has different meanings for different people. A batterer may believe he's showing respect by only threatening rather than actually hitting his partner. Coercion is disrespectful, for sure. A healthy boundary identifies specific actions.

Second, verbalize your boundaries. Speak it. Hoping and expecting others to guess your boundaries leaves you vulnerable and open to more of the same. One client told her sister, "When we talk, I would appreciate it if you didn't interrupt me."

Third, apply consequences. This step seems the most difficult, yet it is perhaps the most effective way to communicate your boundaries. While words are important, though they are only a small part of effective communication. Actions do speak louder than words. And without consequences, other people will just weather the storm of your words, then wait for you to relax and let your guard down, opening the door for them to get their way again.

It's not always easy to establish clear boundaries with family members or loved ones without causing conflict or strain on the relationship because we human beings like getting our way — what we want when we want it. So people, even loved ones, resist having limits applied to their desires. Resistance can manifest as a family member debating or arguing against a new boundary, criticizing the person or boundary, threatening to withhold love and affection, or harming the person setting the boundary physically, financially, etc. Thus, those setting the boundary must prepare for pushback and stand firm in their self-protectiveness.

**Rebuilding Trust**

You might wonder if rebuilding trust and strengthening boundaries is possible after experiencing a breach of trust or violation of boundaries. Lack of trust can lead to increased anxiety and depression in either or both partners. Below are a few tips for rebuilding trust:

1. Identify the specific actions required to create the foundation upon which trust is rebuilt. It's not enough for the violator to say, "I'll work on it," or "I won't do it again". One client was very specific with her fiancé, who cheated. She told him, "I need your passwords, and I need you to be home when you say you will be."

2. The one who violates trust must diligently keep their word, do what they say they will, and say what they do—every time. Or openly communicate when they cannot keep their word due to traffic, illness, etc. And it's vital that the partner who was cheated on refrain from frequently bringing up the infidelity.

3. Both partners must effectively manage their own emotions and communicate authentically.

**Misconceptions**

In my experience, the most common misconception about boundaries is that they are exclusively a women's issue. Women should learn to say no.

Women should know when to leave. Women should recognize abusive people. True. And so should men. While women can learn to better protect and nurture themselves, so can men. If more men and leaders had healthy boundaries, there would be significantly less violence — rape, murder, theft, war, trafficking, abuse, and isms.

The next common misconception is that people believe boundaries are only about saying no. While being able to say no when necessary is important, simply uttering that one word is not enough. Establishing and maintaining healthy boundaries is a complete process that begins before and continues even after saying no. So, if you're in the position of having to say no, then you haven't effectively set or maintained those boundaries.

One client complained about her husband not taking no for an answer. "I've told him no a thousand times, and he just doesn't get it." She didn't realize that 'no' required her to behave her boundaries and not give in. Instead, she empowered him to persist in getting his way by ignoring her own boundaries and giving in. He was relentless in his pursuit of what he wanted, and her compliance only strengthened his resolve.

Another misconception about boundaries is that loved ones should agree to yours. This is often an unrealistic expectation because individuals like to have their way and resist having limits placed upon them, including those they love, admire, adore, depend on, and care for. Identifying, setting, and then affirming your boundaries are required to adequately nurture and protect yourself.

**You Can Do It**

Healthy boundaries nurture and protect you from harmful forces, people, and situations. Your boundaries are your personal, irrefutable, and innate alarm system, monitored by your intuition and available to you 24/7. Healthy boundaries exist with every breath, every "no," and every "yes." Your boundaries are akin to your skin, heart, aura, essence, and every other part of your being. You cannot detach from your boundaries because they live and breathe with and within you. So, your health and wellness depend upon how well you set and affirm your boundaries. And you can do it.

**About the Author**

Glen Alex's work is about health, with careers in social work, writing, charity, therapeutic massage, and tennis. Her transformative mission is to help others be joyful, connected, confident, and complete, the life experience she calls Wellth, which is health + other riches.

Glen's journey in the health space began with boundaries. As a child, she was so engaged by the nuance of interaction—when people smiled, cringed, and when pain crossed their faces. Glen clearly remembers vowing not to be the one to cause another person pain unnecessarily. She saw boundaries respected and boundaries violated, and it stuck. From that, Glen's work expanded to other areas of health, and she developed a unique and no-nonsense perspective to help others lead their healthiest and most joyful life.

Professionally, Glen's experience is well-rounded in health and wellness. She is the Author of the award-winning book *Living In Total Health* and health blogs, a Licensed Clinical Social Worker, a Licensed Massage Therapist, a USPTA Certified Tennis Coach, a Burnalong Instructor, a Wisdom App Top Mentor, the Founder and Executive Director of the former G. Alex Foundation, a Marquis Who's Who Inductee, and the host of the award-winning podcast "The Glen Alex Show."

When not working in one of her many careers, Glen enjoys playing tennis, working out, watching movies, listening to music, and connecting with loved ones.

GlenAlex.com

# Chapter 19

# Embracing Wholeness: The Journey to True Well-Being

Life has an extraordinary way of teaching us that health is much more than a doctor's visit or a balanced meal. It's a complex, intricate web that touches every part of who we are—physically, mentally, and spiritually. My journey toward understanding this wholeness has been deeply personal, shaped by the challenges I've faced, the people I've met, and the lessons I've learned along the way. It's not just an academic pursuit but a way of living, of seeing the body and mind as parts of an interconnected whole that can't be separated.

When I was growing up, health was a simple idea. Like most people, I believed that avoiding illness was enough to be considered "healthy." There were no complex ideas about well-being or balance. Health was a series of steps to follow: eat right, get enough sleep, and go to the doctor when something didn't feel right. It seemed straightforward. But life has a way of showing us the truth through lived experience.

For me, the truth came slowly as I pushed myself harder and harder, watching loved ones struggle through preventable illnesses and realizing that the environment around us—everything from what we eat to where we live—plays a far more significant role in health than I ever imagined.

I wasn't always aware of how intricately connected our bodies, minds, and spirits truly are. My journey to becoming an epidemiologist and professor was paved with moments of intense stress, long hours, and pressure to meet seemingly impossible standards. I remember the fatigue—the kind that doesn't leave you after a night's rest but lingers in your bones, making everything feel heavy. It wasn't just my mind that was worn out; my body was also starting to show the signs. The tension in my shoulders, the chronic headaches, the sense of emotional numbness—it all made me realize that health is not something you can compartmentalize.

It wasn't until I experienced this disconnect firsthand that I truly understood holistic health. I realized that if I didn't take care of myself—physically, mentally, and spiritually—I wouldn't succeed in any of the areas that mattered. It was a wake-up call. The science I had dedicated my life to told me I needed to change.

Nutrition became my first step toward transformation. But it wasn't about some radical diet or quick fix. Instead, it was about recognizing that the food I put into my body was more than just fuel—it was part of a larger connection to myself and the world around me. I began focusing on nutrient-dense, whole foods, and I quickly realized that this was about more than avoiding illness or reaching an ideal weight. It was about feeling alive. Organic, non-GMO foods became a regular part of my life, not just because they were healthier but also because they felt like the right choice for the planet. I started to appreciate the simple acts of washing vegetables, mindful of the pesticides I was rinsing away, aware of the earth from which they came. This seemingly small practice had a ripple effect on every part of my life.

Hydration, something I had once taken for granted, became a daily self-care practice. I learned that it wasn't just about quenching thirst. The water I drank nourished every cell in my body. As I became more intentional about drinking clean, contaminant-free water, I noticed how my energy shifted. I felt clearer, both mentally and physically. Hydrating properly became a symbol of the commitment I was making to my overall well-being. It was a small, daily reminder that I was caring for myself and I was worth the effort.

But food and water were only the beginning. I soon realized that everything around me played a role in my health—the air I breathed, the spaces I lived in, the products I used. I remember the day I made the switch to natural cleaning products. It wasn't a major event, but it was a powerful moment for me. I had always been conscious of the chemicals I put into my body, but until that moment, I hadn't thought much about the ones I used in my home. Switching to non-toxic products felt like a weight lifted off my shoulders, a burden I hadn't even realized I was carrying. Suddenly, I became more aware of the sunlight streaming through my windows, the clutter in my workspace, and the peace that came with simplicity. These small shifts had a profound impact on my overall well-being.

Integrating mind-body practices like mindfulness and meditation into my daily routine was another game changer. At first, it felt unnatural—sitting still, focusing on my breath, allowing myself to simply be. I had always been a person of action, constantly moving forward and always planning the next step. But as I continued to practice mindfulness, I began to see its power. Mindfulness wasn't just a daily ritual; it became a way of life. It taught me to tune into my body's signals, notice when I was pushing myself too hard, and pause when I needed rest. It reminded me that being present, even in the small moments, was just as important as any achievement or milestone.

There's a special kind of clarity that comes from learning to be still, from listening to the quiet parts of yourself that often go unheard in the noise of daily life. Over time, I began to understand that these practices, which I had once dismissed as too simple, were, in fact, my anchor. They kept me grounded in a world that often felt chaotic, reminding me that my health was something to be nurtured, not rushed through.

As I began to embrace these changes, I learned another vital lesson: health is not a solitary endeavor. We cannot thrive in isolation. The relationships we cultivate—the people we love and the communities we belong to—are as essential to our well-being as the food we eat or the water we drink. I've seen it time and time again in my work, in the lives of my students, and in my own life: a sense of belonging, of being part of something bigger than ourselves, has the power to transform us.

These interactions matter whether it's a conversation with a supportive friend, a shared laugh with family, or even a moment of connection with a stranger. They feed us in ways that go beyond the physical. I've witnessed how community can heal, provide strength during difficult times, and lift us when we feel alone. That's why I believe so deeply in the importance of community—not just in a professional sense but in a deeply personal way.

As a professor, I've always encouraged my students to see health not just as a set of biological processes but as something much larger—something that touches every aspect of our lives. I want them to understand that their choices, the connections they foster, and the environments they create will shape their well-being in ways they may not even realize. Holistic health isn't just about avoiding illness or ticking off boxes on a checklist. It's about living in harmony with ourselves, others, and the world around us.

Ultimately, holistic health is all about balance. It's about recognizing that every choice we make, from the food we eat to how we spend our time, affects us in ways we might not see immediately. It's about living in tune with our bodies, minds, and spirits, knowing that each part of ourselves is connected to the others. It's about embracing both the joys and the challenges that life brings and understanding that health is not a destination but a journey.

When I reflect on the lessons I've learned throughout my life, I am reminded of how far I've come. Holistic health has transformed me—not just in how I care for myself but also in how I view the world. It has taught me that health is not something we can achieve through quick fixes or external measures but something that comes from within. It's the result of the choices we make every day, the habits we cultivate, and the love we show ourselves and those around us.

As I continue this journey, I hope my story can inspire others to embark on their own path toward true well-being. When we take the time to care for ourselves wholly and deeply, we open the door to a life that is not just lived but truly experienced—a life rich with balance, connection, and meaning—a life where health is not simply about avoiding illness but about embracing the fullness of who we are.

**About the Author**

Dr. Tia Warrick is a professor, epidemiologist, and clinical trial consultant with expertise in statistics, data analysis, study design, and research writing. She holds a Doctor of Health Science, a Master in Public Health Epidemiology, and a Bachelor of Biology. Tia has published two acclaimed books: the award-winning *Burst the Bubble,* set to be featured on the Times Square Nasdaq billboard, and *What the Heal*, a memoir detailing her life's journey through challenges. She also plays a key role in managing communication for public health programs. Outside of work, Tia enjoys cooking, singing/songwriting, traveling, playing volleyball, and participating in charitable events.

lesousconsulting.com
drwarrick@lesousconsultingllc.com

# Chapter 20

## Homeopathic Medicine: Tiny Doses, Big Impact

Maria Bohle

I often get asked how I became interested in Homeopathic Medicine. Thirty years ago, during a very stressful time in my life, I contracted Lyme disease. The disease had become systemic, leading to neurological complaints, memory impairment, chronic fatigue, and bodily pain. After three years on antibiotics with no improvement, I sought out alternative therapy. I came across a sign for a homeopath and decided to try it. After a two-hour interview, I was given a homeopathic remedy that made my Lyme symptoms disappear like an ice cube in the sand on a hot, sunny July beach. This experience led me to pursue more knowledge about homeopathy. Today, thanks to homeopathic treatment, I can work long hours pursuing my passions. Two years ago, I even received a black belt in karate, and I am currently working on my second-degree black belt.

Homeopathic means 'similar to the pathology,' so homeopathic medicine treats the patient's symptoms with a substance that can cause those same symptoms in a healthy person. Actually, this is how homeopathic medicines are identified. Homeopaths find healthy people to take their highly reduced (attenuated) medicines and record the symptoms the medicines cause. This is called a 'proving' from the old word 'pruf' for how bread bakers tested or 'proofed' the yeast to be sure it would cause the bread to rise.

The patient is provided with an appropriate dosage of the medicinal substance, intending to achieve curative results while minimizing toxicity by decreasing the concentration of active ingredients. The amount is reduced enough to be safe and gentle, ensuring the patient's safety and comfort but active enough to engage the body's homeostatic mechanism.

**An Example of a Homeostatic Mechanism**

A patient presents with a headache pain level of 7. It is important to understand that the body may use that pain to maintain its internal balance. If a substance, such as an opioid, is given to reduce the headache, the pain is relieved. However, the underlying cause of the headache remains unaddressed, and the body may compensate by increasing the intensity of the headache. This can lead to a situation where higher and higher doses of the medicine are needed to control the head pain. Homeopaths recognize that when someone experiences a headache with a pain level of 7, it indicates what the body needs. In response, the homeopath selects a highly diluted medicinal substance that can produce similar symptoms to the patient's headache, ensuring a personalized and tailored treatment. The homeopath also takes into consideration the cause of the headache, whether it's because of dehydration, hypertension, high stress levels, exhaustion, or other reasons, and ensures that this cause is part of the overall picture of symptoms. Following that, the patient is given the corresponding substance, which is referred to as a 'remedy'.

Although this represents a greatly simplified approach to homeopathic medicine, a comprehensive understanding of the more than 5,000 available remedies can significantly augment the level of study required to achieve mastery in this field.

Symptom totality itself is also a major study. Homeopaths consider the patient's family history, medical history, and exactly how the disease manifests within that patient. Homeopathy is considered a remarkably safe treatment when practiced by a proficient and well-versed practitioner.

Instead of employing active medicinal substances in increasing quantities, the potency of homeopathic medicine is determined by its dilutions.

In essence, the process dilutes and energizes the remedies. Most medicines are soluble in water, and water, being a universal solvent, wraps around any impurities, forming a molecular configuration. If a small vial of a medicinal substance dissolved in water is shaken, the effect is similar to rubbing a balloon on a piece of clothing and then sticking the balloon to the wall. The energized electrons or static electricity will hold it there for some time. Except water has a memory. Excited electrons in an aqueous form retain that memory, especially when shaken in a glass bottle. Dilute and shake (succuss) systematically, and the homeopathic remedy reduces the molecules but creates a highly energetic molecular configuration replicating the entire remedy structure. It can go in deeply and safely return a diseased body to normal function. Remedies can hold their energy for years. There are homeopathic remedies from the Civil War era that still work.

I witness daily miracles in my homeopathic clinic and have several file cabinets full of satisfied patients previously considered "Failed Mainstream Medical Cases." However, not every patient who leaves my office can be viewed as a miracle. I refer patients to mainstream medical practitioners, chiropractors, physical therapists, and other complementary healthcare providers based on what the patient needs. Our medical goal is to help ease pain and distress in our patients. As Hahnemann said, we aim to "free our patients to get on with their higher order of existence."

We hate hearing or saying, 'We have exhausted all reasonable possibilities, and there is nothing more we can do for you.' The next step is to make the patient as comfortable as possible. This is when we want to explore another plan of action. What medical treatments or modalities can we pursue for our patients?

Step into complementary and alternative medicine, where we can provide hope and a plan of action for the future. Recent studies show that nearly 83% of the population uses some form of complementary medicine, even paying out of pocket for it.

**Clinical Nutrition:** Clinical nutrition relies on medical tests to assess the biochemical pathways to disease. By understanding the nutrient needs of specific organs and tissues, clinical nutritionists provide those nutrients to maintain and sustain the diseased organ under the burden of pathology to improve function and attempt to provide the necessary components for repair. Deficiencies in digestive enzymes, which prevent the amino acid tyrosine from being released from the patient's food, can cause hypothyroidism, for instance. It can also be caused by deficiencies of iodine or the body's inability to use iodine and formulate the thyroid hormone when necessary trace elements are missing.

**Herbal Medicine:** Herbal Medicine is another nutritive strategy with medicinal components in a natural balance. It takes the long view of stimulating and 'feeding' organs and tissues. The herbs' components possess antibiotic and nutritional properties, and many can be safely used over an extended period.

A perfect example is Hawthorn tincture or extract for cardiac issues. Hawthorn is generally non-toxic and can be used alongside cardiac and hypertensive medicines over a long period (a year or more if needed). This herb slowly supports the heart, cleans out cholesterol in the vascular system, and reduces blood pressure.

**Homeopathic Medicine:** Homeopathic medicine is becoming more popular and is being included in national healthcare options in many countries. It takes a holistic approach to treating medical conditions using highly diluted medicinal substances as catalytic agents. This approach relies heavily on subjective information, focusing on how the patient reacts to the illness rather than the common symptoms. While the common pathological symptoms are important and considered when determining the medicinal substances, the specific remedy is tailored based on the individual patient's strange, rare, and peculiar symptoms, as well as the cause of the disorder and the patient's mental and emotional challenges.

Training in homeopathy for chronic diseases requires thorough training, and the patient interview is very time-consuming. A recent case in my student clinic involved a young man with necrotizing pancreatitis who sought help at our clinic as a last resort. His prognosis was grim, and his doctors had informed him that there were no further treatment options available. The patient was experiencing chronic pain, had significant fluid discharge from a pancreatic drain, and was in a high level of discomfort. Although initially skeptical about homeopathy, the patient's pain has decreased by more than half, the drainage tube has been removed, and although there is still some drainage, it has significantly reduced. He has also regained around 60 pounds of the weight he had lost.

Complementary medicine is not intended to replace mainstream medicine. Still, it can complement traditional treatments, especially for early-stage diseases or cases that do not respond to standard therapies for various reasons.

I had to study, and The British Institute of Homeopathy (BIH) brought the studies to me and over 15,000 students since 1987. The British Institute still provides a professional homeopathic program to people who want to become homeopaths. Former BIH students practice all over the world today. I started teaching for the British Institute, and when the owner retired, I bought the school. A few years later, I traveled to India with two advanced students to study clinical practice under the guidance of a very astute homeopath, Dr. Ashok Borkar, from Goa, India. Dr. Borkar, now the British Institute's Clinical Training Director, has been in practice for over 25 years and, along with his staff of 10 homeopaths, sees 60 patients daily, six days a week. Over 500 million people worldwide depend on homeopathic medicine for their healthcare. Homeopathy is a part of frontline healthcare for many governments, including Mexico, which has recently added homeopathy to its national healthcare system.

As you can now see, Homeopaths work with the immune system, not against it. Homeopathy has been the most rewarding pursuit of my life. I have taught hundreds of students how to practice this gentle yet effective branch of medicine. I hope you will consider it too.

## About the Author

Maria T. Bohle discovered her passion for herbs and healing at Harvard University in the 1960s. In the early 1970s, she and her husband started the Herb Garden business in Southern New Jersey, specializing in growing culinary and medicinal herbs. They naturally maintain farm animals, poultry, and flowers without using pesticides, insecticides, or chemicals.

Following successful treatment for Lyme disease, she was eager to learn more about homeopathy and enrolled in the British Institute of Homeopathy under the direction of Dr. Trevor Cook. She graduated from BIH with the highest honors and earned the Hahnemann Award for excellence. Maria received a UK diploma and a doctorate in homeopathic medicine, both recognized in the UK.

Maria completed her homeopathic postgraduate studies with several renowned homeopaths, including David Little, Massimo Mangialavori, Dr. A.U. Ramakrishnan, Alize Timmerman, Will Taylor, Jeremy Sherr, Sheliagh Creasy, and most recently, Dr. Ashok Borkar from India.

Maria has over 26 years of experience as a nationally certified professional homeopath (CHC) specializing in herbal medicine and running a private homeopathic practice. She holds degrees in Nutrition and Clinical Nutrition and a PhD in the Health Sciences. Additionally, she has been trained in Bach Flower Therapy and Gemmotherapy, is a Reiki Master, and has held an EMT certification (and practiced) for 15 years. She is a life member of the EHT Volunteer Fire Company Auxiliary and a life member and past secretary of the Atlantic County Agriculture Extension Executive Board. She also holds a first-degree Black Belt in Tang So Do Karate and is working on her second-degree black belt.

In 2001, she became the Director of BIH USA and established the current office in Egg Harbor Township while maintaining a thriving homeopathic practice. Upon Dr. Cook's retirement, Maria purchased BIH and moved the headquarters to New Jersey in 2010.

In addition to her homeopathic degrees, Maria holds a degree from Harvard University, completed her Master's in Clinical Nutrition, and has a PhD in Natural Sciences from Westbrook University.

mtbohle@gmail.com

# Chapter 21

# Trauma-Informed Care within the Wellness Movement

Ernest Ellender

Compared to the rat race of modern American existence, with its medical "sick care" model that most people unknowingly adhere to in their daily lives, the wellness lifestyle offers superior health, happiness, and longevity. More and more people are flocking to this wellness lifestyle in anticipation of the wonderful benefits it delivers to its practitioners. Let us take a moment here to address a challenging obstacle that can thwart a person's efforts to achieve their wellness goals: childhood trauma and its resulting chronic stress.

Before you skip this chapter with the self-dismissive statement, "I was not abused, so this doesn't apply to me," hang in with me here and consider the following: "70% of adults in the U.S. have experienced some type of traumatic event at least once in their lives...In public behavioral health, over 90% of clients have experienced trauma" (National Council 2022). Let us further clarify that you need not have experienced childhood physical or sexual abuse to be included in the traumatized 70 percent. The Adverse Childhood Experiences (ACE) Study (Felitti et al. 1998) demonstrated that just one childhood trauma, like experiencing your parents' divorce or having an addict in your childhood household, is enough to negatively impact your adult health for the rest of your life.

The key concept to understand about childhood trauma is that these painful childhood experiences can cause an individual to become stuck in *survival mode,* leading to a chronic state of heightened anxiety that is antithetical to long-term health and wellness. This survival mode exhausts the body, as its evolutionary purpose is to supercharge our athletic functioning for short periods to help us deal with life-threatening situations. Once the danger has passed, we no longer need survival mode; it is time for the body to return to a relaxed state for recovery and preparation for the next danger that comes along. Being stuck in survival mode for long periods is taxing to the body. Complete, optimal recovery becomes impossible, leaving these people with many medical issues, poor health, and shorter-than-average life spans.

Regulated by the central nervous system, the human body responds to its environment by alternating between two states. In safe environments, the human body typically remains in parasympathetic nervous system dominance, also known as *rest-and-digest* mode. In this state, blood flow to the stomach, brain, and extremities is increased for optimal digestion of foods and repair of cells throughout the entire body. The moment a perceived danger enters the environment, survival mode is activated, and the sympathetic nervous system takes over to prepare the body for the survival responses of fight, flight, freeze, or fawn. Blood flow is drawn away from the temporarily unnecessary digestive tract and prefrontal cortex, rushing instead to the body parts most important for survival of short-term danger: the chest cavity (heart, lungs) and the base of the brain (sensory, emotion, and motor centers). The evolutionary message is clear: "Don't think...act!"

How, then, does a child get stuck in chronic states of anxiety? When encountering either short, intensely traumatic events (physical abuse, sexual abuse, abandonment, witnessing physical abuse of a parent) or prolonged periods of low-grade fear (parental separation or divorce, aggressive verbal arguments, sibling or parent in addiction), a child's brain recognizes the danger of the situation and then comes up with its own subconscious rules for how to survive it. Because these directives involve survival, they are highly resistant to change: the child carries these subconscious *trauma lies*, which quietly guide their behaviors into adulthood. Some examples of trauma lies include the following:

- "The world is dangerous, so I must be ready to fight (or run) at all times."
- "To survive, I must placate dangerous aggressors by giving them what they want."
- "People are (dangerous/manipulative/unreliable), so I must survive on my own."

As adults, these childhood trauma survivors are often unaware of the significant extent to which their trauma lies continues to impact their adult functioning. When a colleague at work shirks their duties, for example, causing problems for the trauma survivor, the survivor may refrain from advocating for themself because their childhood trauma lie subconsciously reminds them, "People are dangerous. To survive, I must remain as unseen as possible." Even though resentments build for the survivor as they suffer at work and continue to get passed over for promotions and pay raises, the survivor remains frozen in their deep-seated fear and chronic survival mode. Some survivors are very aware that they suffer from chronic anxiety (even if they don't make the connection to their childhood experiences). In contrast, others feel "normal" for most of the week but instantly shift into survival mode when triggered by something that reminds them of their childhood trauma.

How do these survivors exit their chronic survival mode? How can they stop being triggered by reminders of their past traumas? These are great questions that require significant study to answer thoroughly, but let us first consider whose job it is to help survivors heal. The lingering consequences of childhood traumas are so complex, challenging, and often counterintuitive that survivors wanting to address their childhood issues directly are well advised to seek the assistance of professional clinicians who are educated and practiced in appropriate treatment protocols. While loving family members and friends may offer well-intended advice like "Try to forget that it happened," educated professionals understand why survivors cannot simply "get over it," no matter how tough they are.

**Trauma-specific services** include interventions and therapeutic services intended to treat the symptoms and conditions resulting from traumatizing events directly. Therapists, counselors, psychiatrists, life coaches, and other professionals can seek out education and training on empirically validated treatments shown through research to be effective at treating trauma issues. There are literally hundreds of ways to treat trauma directly, but some of the better-known empirically validated treatments include trauma-focused cognitive behavioral therapy (TF-CBT), dialectical behavior therapy (DBT), eye movement desensitization and reprocessing (EMDR), somatic therapy, medication management, narrative exposure therapy, and prolonged exposure therapy. With proper treatment under the guidance of these professionals, trauma survivors can directly reduce their trauma symptoms and learn skills that help them successfully manage lingering issues.

Most wellness providers and professionals seek to provide healing services to all people, including childhood trauma survivors. Without going to an additional 6–12 years of schooling to earn the degrees needed to offer *trauma-specific services*, wellness providers can dive into the much more accessible practice of providing *trauma-informed care*.

**Trauma-informed care** is a movement that seeks to ensure that the environments and services offered are based on knowledge of the impact of trauma, making them welcoming and engaging for all—trauma survivors included. In other words, these services do not aim to directly treat a survivor's trauma symptoms; instead, they deliver other types of services (medical, fitness, sales, nutrition, yoga, massage, etc.) in such a fashion that they do not push away the survivor by accidentally triggering their trauma symptoms. Being sensitive to the unique challenges of trauma survivors requires that trauma-informed care practitioners understand the impact of trauma, be aware of appropriate recovery options, and recognize the signs and symptoms of trauma in their clients. These providers can actively avoid re-traumatizing their clients by integrating this knowledge base into their policies and practices. Things like office decorations and staff interactions can lead a trauma survivor to feel either more motivated to engage with the service at hand or anxious to disengage. The integration of trauma-informed care in a workplace typically results in keeping the trauma survivors in the group engaged for more time, treatment, and activities—in such environments, survivors often feel safe enough to stay.

**Case study.** During graduate school, I participated in a study at the Veterans Affairs in Palo Alto, California, in which head researcher Julie Weitlauf, PhD (2003) was studying the effectiveness of a women's self-defense course intended to directly treat PTSD in female military veterans. Dr. Weitlauf replicated a similar pilot study at another VA facility, resulting in positive and problematic findings. She hypothesized that the reason for the problematic parts of the first study was that the martial artists hired to teach the self-defense course had not been trained in trauma-informed care. These martial artists undoubtedly had great intentions to help research participants, but they were uneducated on trauma symptoms and triggers, as well as how to respond constructively when participants were triggered by self-defense activities. To address this concern, Dr. Weitlauf assembled our treatment team from therapists who also had martial arts training. I was included because of my expertise in Brazilian Jiu-Jitsu (BJJ), and I worked with her team to instruct several cohorts of the study over four years' time, during which I saw Dr. Weitlauf's trauma-informed strategy pay off repeatedly. The study participants regularly experienced distress of some kind, from slight apprehension to full-blown panic, when triggered by something that reminded them of their traumas. Once triggered, participants were expertly tended to by one or more of the therapist-instructors such that they were able to rejoin the group activity after a brief therapeutic intervention (typically 2–10 minutes). The results of this study showed significant improvement over the prior pilot study, demonstrating the effectiveness of integrating trauma-informed care principles.

Learning how to offer trauma-informed care can seem daunting to those new to the concept, so let us demystify the process. For the sake of simplicity, we can boil the many components of trauma-informed care down to two basic elements: a welcoming, safe atmosphere and key referrals. Many survivors have learned in their stressful childhoods that their health and happiness are not important to other people in their lives. An inviting attitude, patience with struggling clients, transparency of procedures, responsiveness to client inquiries, and practices that empower clients can be combined to establish a safe and welcoming environment that promotes trust between survivors and trauma-informed wellness practitioners. Safety and trust enable survivors to relax as they engage with the wellness activities and personnel. Staff patience and trustworthiness send the nonverbal message that survivors' words and presence are valued by the service providers.

As the survivor experiences this welcoming and safe environment, they often begin to open up and discuss their rough past. Many survivors have experienced "crazy" human behaviors and struggle with discussing them due to society's discomfort with taboo topics like sexual abuse, domestic violence, incest, and addiction. The trauma-informed wellness practitioner remembers that it is not their job to directly treat their client's trauma symptoms, and they take care to offer their clients nonjudgmental validation, practical support, and encouragement to seek professional help. With practice and trauma-informed training, wellness providers can become skilled in both welcoming survivors' engagement and offering them key referrals to professionals who *can* directly treat their trauma symptoms. Each successful attempt to connect a childhood trauma survivor with trauma-specific service professionals is indeed a very big deal—it can have a positive impact on that individual's entire family for generations to come!

Consistent training, academic study, and self-education pave the way for achieving trauma-informed status for each wellness provider and facility. Wellness facilities can offer their staff access to quality educational resources so that the entire staff can collaborate to become increasingly trauma-informed. An internet search for "online classes for trauma-informed care" will be met with an array of structured options for individuals and organizations. These options can be a wonderful start: they typically offer a comprehensive introduction to understanding the total process. Once this big picture is decently understood, deeper dives into individual concepts (such as reducing trauma triggers, responding to the triggered survivor, and maintaining healthy boundaries) can further providers' education and competence in that area. Less formally, each wellness provider can self-educate by reading books or research journals, watching free online content, and taking courses on the topic.

The concept of healthy boundaries presents an example of the tricky grounds that trauma-informed education can address. It's only natural for individuals raised in unhealthy childhood homes to have a poor understanding of healthy boundaries. Relationships with these survivors can rapidly become unhealthy when a well-intended wellness practitioner is drawn into the pain and chaos of a survivor's turbulent inner world. However, as the practitioner learns about healthy emotional, cognitive, and behavioral boundaries, they can make their interactions with the struggling survivor more therapeutic by explaining safe, structured boundaries in plain words and adhering to them: "While I can't give you money to help with your painfully difficult financial situation, let's spend some time now looking into local services that can help you. We can make some calls together!"

In summary, becoming a trauma-informed wellness provider is a powerful practice, considering that statistically, the majority (upwards of 70%) of clients will have experienced at least one impactful trauma in their lives. Keeping survivors engaged with trauma-informed wellness services, in addition to connecting them with trauma-specific services, can help them achieve their greatest health and happiness outcomes. Getting started on this path has never been easier with access to books and online educational opportunities. We are all in this together, so let's keep improving the reach and effectiveness of wellness services...for everyone!

## About the Author

Ernest Ellender worked in clinical psychology, life coaching, and martial arts for over 20 years before authoring his first book, *This Is How We Heal from Painful Childhoods: A Practical Guide for Healing Past Intergenerational Stress and Trauma*. In this book, Ernest offers his empowering curriculum to readers worldwide who wish to heal from their past and develop the knowledge and skills necessary for success in relationships and life. Nowadays, Ernest offers professional life coaching services while also promoting his new book. In his free time, you will find him traveling or enjoying the bayous and beaches of South Louisiana with family and friends.

ernestellenderphd.com

eellender@gmail.com

# Chapter 22

# Loss: One Common Thread

Donna Kincheloe

Healthcare organizations provide mandated education to staff by assigning webinars and computerized training sessions. The information provided on cyber security, fire safety, protocols and policies, and new care delivery models is excellent. However, I believe something is missing that has the propensity to improve the well-being and health of staff, patients, and families.

Educating employees on the one common thread promised in this life can change perspectives, provide hope, and offer ways to embrace a more compassionate, nonjudgmental culture. The often neglected topic is loss.

**Consider the Truths about Loss**

- Loss is universal, and no one is exempt.
- Loss affects people from every country, regardless of social or financial status or faith tradition. It is extremely personal, and everyone will respond in their own way.
- Loss is not a comparison study. My sweet Vizsla died unexpectedly. A friend miscarried sixty years ago. As we discussed our losses, she scolded me and said, "The death of your dog doesn't come close to the loss of my baby." And I kindly let her know it is terribly hurtful to demean another person's loss.

Always be careful not to reduce or diminish another's loss because you believe yours is greater. Choose a listening ear and heartfelt concern, not judgment.

- Losses in life can be tiny or huge.
- A loss-intensity ruler does not exist. A twelve-inch ruler is a consistent measuring tool, complete with equality and universal agreement. The inch on my ruler is the same as yours. Loss intensity can only be ranked by the one living the loss.
- Some people experience more loss in life than others, and coping with the scenarios may have a longer-lasting effect. Another perspective is that some who have experienced many losses may have applied lessons learned and gained grit, giving them credibility to educate and encourage others with empathy, not sympathy.
- Loss is an unexpected event that begins with an end.

**Loss Can Carry Universal Change**

Loss in the acute care setting was never more evident than during the COVID-19 pandemic. Like many hospitals, nurses were offered a high bonus to sign up for sixteen weeks, working extra twelve-hour shifts. Money flowed freely, and many signed up for multiple contracts. Code Blue and rapid response blared daily over the intercom. Loss lingered around every hallway and corridor. Hearts grew heavy as spiritual, emotional, and physical stamina fell fast and hard. Every unit became an ICU.

A large post-COVID-19 research study from the National Council of State Boards of Nursing reported that about 100,000 nurses left the workforce from 2021 to 2023. The main reasons for exiting included stress, burnout, and retirement. Add to that number the alarming future projections of greater than 600,000, indicating the intent to leave nursing by 2027 for the same reasons.

Loss came. Nurses left. Before they did, many sought help to deal with the situation and the mental health counseling center was overwhelmed. One experienced nurse attended an appointment, and the new counselor said, “I am so glad you are here. I am new and really have no idea what you are experiencing. Perhaps you can help me understand and know what to tell the rest of the nurses coming to see me.”

That nurse sought help to cope with loss and ended up having to give more of herself when there was little left to give.

Being aware can help people prepare. If staff created a loss lifeline and documented their losses and lessons learned before a crisis, this activity may reveal strengths and weaknesses. Identifying specific ways to cope with loss will impact the lives of patients, co-workers, and family. Waiting until after an event to educate and equip is a practice built in futility. Understanding the truths of loss before loss is much more beneficial.

A preacher once asked my friend this question, “What would you do if you went home tonight and found your home engulfed by flames and everything you owned destroyed?’”

Years later, to his surprise, his apartment was ablaze. My friend said, “My mind went back to my imaginary fire. I already knew things could be replaced, but life couldn’t.”

The imaginary fire became a reality, but the pre-preparation lessened a burning anger reaction and a woe-is-me moment.

**Types of Loss**

Abuse, addiction, alcoholism, bankruptcy, being bullied, broken relationships, parental divorce, dysfunctional family system, displacement, death of loved ones (including pets), disappointment, failing courses, being fired, illness, infertility, miscarriage, rape, stolen identity, suicide.

We can place these losses into categories of unhealthy relationships, physical ailments, mental and emotional angst, and death.

**Acknowledge the Truth About Loss**

Identifying the manifestations in ourselves or others helps obtain and maintain well-being.

Loss triggers feelings. When sadness, helplessness, anger, confusion, or brain fog appear in others' lives, we may need to gently inquire if loss is the culprit. Ignoring warning signs harms everyone.

Since loss is such a personal experience, it is important to know that some people choose not to deal with it. Some people do not like to experience feelings they do not have control over. Some numb the feelings with drugs and alcohol. Others throw themselves into work and isolate themselves.

**Loss and Grief**

Loss is not a loner. Grief accompanies loss.

Grief is the emotional response to loss.

A discussion about loss must include the dance partner named grief. A stark paradox exists between the two definitions.

Loss begins with an end.

Grief is the emotional response to loss with an indeterminate end.

Imagine grief as a disorganized play. When the curtain goes up, the players are unsure of their lines. We expect the scenes to be sequenced, yet they lack order. Most playwrights ensure a timely show, yet once this play begins, it feels like it will never end. The stage is dim. The plot lacks focus, leaving the audience pondering a multitude of questions. When the curtain finally falls, you exit empty. You wonder if you can find your way home.

Such is grief. People do not know what to say. The grief stages are not sequential. Grief does not come with a time limit. The light in life is gone. All is dark. A barrage of questions pounce: Why me? Why us? Why now? What next? Where is God?

**The Right Words**

Knowing the right words to say when someone is experiencing loss is difficult. Pulling from critical incident stress management and grief counseling, these tips may help.

Please don't say:

"I know how you feel" (because you don't)!

"He/She is in a better place."

"You should be over this by now."

"Buck up! Stop your crying!"

"This is all your fault!"

"God needed him/her more."

There is power in silent presence. Be mindful of a person's preference to touch. Some love hugs, some don't. Don't bring up God unless they do. Be honest in your conversation. "I have no idea what you are going through." "I wish I could take away your pain, but I can't."

Be aware that when the barrage of 'why' questions fly, don't feel you need to respond with an answer when there is none.

**Compassionate Responses**

After 9/11, I attended a conference on critical incident stress management, and the presenter discussed the right words to say. A young man stood and agreed, "You're right. Three weeks ago, my wife miscarried. The right words from a nurse gave me strength when she said, this baby has been loved all her life."

Jim, a nursing student, shared this story. During visitation at the funeral home, a gentleman approached, shook his hand, and said, "I want you to know your grandma has studied for this final all her life. I know she passed."

My neighbor lost her husband and stressed the sweetest friends were those who just sat beside her and said nothing. They let her talk when she felt like it. They didn't have to fill the air with awkward words.

Lois, a woman of strong faith, taught a valuable lesson. Relaxing in the captain's chair in my dining room, she said, "Donna, I want you to know what I love about you. You are the only one who lets me talk about dying. No one else lets me even bring it up. Other friends might as well put duct tape on my mouth. They stop me quickly and say, 'God will heal you. We are praying hard. You're not going to die.' But not you. Granted, we both are nurses. I know I am dying, and you do, too. You are as comfortable with the truth as I am. I know you will care about what I want and don't want. I can tell you precisely what to pray for. I don't want to die struggling to breathe. I want to die easy. I am going to go to heaven and be with Jesus."

**Grief Model**

An overview of the five stages of the Kubler-Ross Grief Model includes denial, anger, bargaining, depression, and acceptance.

Denial is the initial natural defense mechanism to shed the shock.

Anger is a purposeful emotion that may surprise you and others. The directionality may be inappropriate, but expressing anger can be helpful. My calm, light-hearted husband lost a job due to downsizing. When he took a butter knife and began whacking his crusty dinner roll into crumbs while at a restaurant with friends, we watched in horror until he busted out laughing, and so did we.

Bargaining with God is common. "Lord, if you let me live until I see my grandbaby, I promise I will stop smoking now." And sometimes, people dwell on the "if only" statements that connect regret and blame to their actions or inactions. "If only I took my disease seriously and took my meds as ordered."

Depression is when reality hits and covers a person with a blanket of sadness. Physical symptoms may pop up. The motivation to get out of bed or engage in everyday activities disappears. The main difference between clinical depression and this stage of grief requires attention to the degree and longevity. Over time, depression of grief should lessen.

Acceptance is associated with time, adjusting, and moving ahead at whatever pace you set. Over time, the emotions of anger, guilt, and numbness will incrementally ease. Remember, baby steps are steps.

We all know grief and loss are among life's guarantees. Healthcare organizations and professionals can empower staff through educational sessions to help increase awareness about loss. When people know the right words to say, embrace the value of understanding loss, and recognize the stages of grief, a compassionate sensitivity can grow. Well-being and health will improve for all.

**About the Author**

Dr. Donna Kincheloe was a bedside nurse, clinical instructor, and preceptor for forty-four years. She held certifications in critical care, medical-surgical nursing, heart failure, and critical incident stress management. She secured over $40,000 of grant funds for hundreds of nurses who gained access to online courses to obtain certifications.

In 2018 the Journal of Clinical Nursing published her statistically significant spiritual care research project. Dr. Donna is a peer reviewer for The Journal of Christian Nursing, volunteers to speak at various community events, and is a guest lecturer for the University of Southern Indiana and IVY Tech Community College, presenting Loss, Grief, Dying, and Spiritual Care to nursing students.

She received the 2024 Golden Scroll Memoir of the Year award for *A Life Just Like Mine: How God and Nursing Turned Past Pain into Present Peace*. Her book *I Never Walk the Halls Alone* sold over 3,000 copies and is now available as an audiobook on over fifty platforms. True stories of patients, families, and friends reveal the importance of heart-to-heart communication and compassionate caregiving.

Dr. Donna and her husband, Allen, live in Indiana and share a love for gardening. She also loves knitting, baking, singing, speaking, blogging, and selling at bazaars.

walkthehalls.com

drdonnakdnp@gmail.com

# Chapter 23

# Healthy Adoptive Families Start with Self-Reflection

Tom Tracy

***"We look at adoption as a very sacred exchange. It was not done lightly on either side." – Jamie Lee Curtis***

*Chapter Author's Note: There are many types of adoption, each worthy of its own discussion. This chapter is based on the author's experience growing his family through private, domestic adoption, and it is written from this perspective.*

Despite being taught about the "birds and the bees" in our middle school health education classes, little is done to prepare us for what lies ahead when family creation must take a different path. Families created through adoption are never "unplanned" or by "accident." It is an intentional decision that starts with a willingness to embrace all the nuanced elements associated with the decision to adopt. In addition to the typical hurdles and milestones associated with parenting and childhood development, adoptive families face unique circumstances that must also be acknowledged to promote healthy social and emotional development. Understanding some of these areas can help professionals develop a deeper level of empathy for adoptive families, creating an environment that allows for more effective support and care.

## The Statistics

Any conversation about adoption should start with first understanding the prevalence of adoption in the United States. According to the Adoption Network

(https://adoptionnetwork.com/adoption-myths-facts/domestic-us-statistics/),

- 4.5 million Americans have been adopted, representing about 7% of the total U.S. population.
- As much as 1 out of every 25 U.S. families with children have adopted.
- 95% of domestic adoptions are open (some level of contact with the child's biological family).
- 25% of adopted children are of a different race, culture, or ethnicity than their adoptive parents.

## Our Story

We are a gay couple. Both of us always wanted to have children. Two years after we married, we decided it was time to grow our family beyond the two dogs and two cats that were already occupying space in our hearts and home. It was time to explore having children.

Like so many other couples who pursue their goal of creating a family through "alternative" methods, our journey began with lots of research! We educated ourselves about foster care, adoption (both domestic and international), foster-to-adopt, surrogacy, our legal rights and protections, and, of course, the cost. With just a few clicks of a mouse, we found ourselves at a virtual smorgasbord of information. This was followed by attending multiple information sessions, discussions with attorneys and physicians, conversations with LGBTQIA+ advocacy organizations, and sorting through stacks and stacks of brochures intended to "make the decision easier." Newsflash—it's not easy! In fact, learning about alternative methods to create a family can feel like you're traveling cross-country with a GPS repeatedly shouting "rerouting" while trying to read a 20-year-old tattered and coffee-stained roadmap, all as you nervously watch a gas gauge precariously inching closer to "E."

Armed with our information, we gripped the wheel, put our foot on the gas, and took the fork in the road that read "Adoption, This Way." Little did we know that was just the beginning of even more questions to explore and decisions to be made. What type of adoption did we want to pursue - domestic or international? Foster-to-adopt or private adoption? Should we use a not-for-profit agency or a for-profit one? Did that matter? Do we attempt to find a birth mother on our own? Would the child's birth state allow for both of us to adopt, or would one of us need to be the "primary parent" followed by a "second parent adoption" later? Every option had its own share of fairytale-like happily-ever-after endings. Still, it seemed there were just as many nightmare stories of failed or "disrupted" adoptions, some of which left prospective adoptive parents in financial ruin and absolutely heartbroken. Have I said yet that the decision to build a family through alternative methods isn't easy and can be overwhelming, especially for LGBTQIA+ prospective parents?

Somehow, we muddled through, turning left here and right there, each decision leading us to where we are today – two daughters who became part of our family through separate private, domestic, transracial infant adoptions. While the journey wasn't easy, I can honestly say, like all other parents on the planet, our kids are the light of our lives. Our kitchen is wallpapered with drawings of hearts and rainbows, our floors are littered with Legos ™ and other small toys that attack our feet during the wee hours, but most of all, our days are brighter and fuller (despite our nights being shorter – thanks, sleep regression!). And we'd have it no other way!

## Fostering a Resilient & Emotionally Healthy Adoptive Family

We all want our families and our children to be healthy and strong. As parents, we'll go to the ends of the Earth to benefit our children. This is universal. However, adoptive families require additional tools in the parental toolkit to promote resilience and positive emotional development. Filling that toolkit begins the moment a couple decides to adopt and is a lifelong commitment that involves self-reflection and the courage to address personal biases to instill a strong sense of identity in adoptive children.

## Pre-Adoption

There are some big questions about sensitive topics that prospective adoptive parents must answer for themselves. Unlike couples who conceive through the "traditional" method, prospective adoptive parents will find they need to honestly reflect on their opinions and beliefs around such subjects as:

- *Race* – comfort adopting a child of a different race; to what degree are the prospective adoptive parents willing to help a child stay connected to their own race to develop a strong sense of racial identity?

- *Mental health* – biological family history may genetically predispose a child to mental illness; what, if any, diagnoses are beyond the comfort level of the prospective adoptive parents? Are the comfort levels different for depression versus schizophrenia, for instance?

- *Alcohol & Substance use* – does the prospective adoptive family feel comfortable with a baby who has been exposed to drugs or alcohol? What about newborns who will need to go through withdrawal upon birth?

- *Incest/Rape* – does the circumstance of the child's conception make a difference to the prospective parent? Are certain circumstances more "acceptable" than others?

- *Open Adoption* – there are many degrees of open adoption, ranging from the exchange of letters to in-person visits with the biological family. What a birth mother requests may be different than what a prospective adoptive parent feels comfortable with.

As if the prospect of becoming a parent wasn't daunting enough, having to think about these areas and then reveal your answers to an adoption agency can be intimidating and leave prospective adoptive parents feeling vulnerable, to say the least.

This self-awareness / personal bias inventory isn't just a "check-the-box exercise;" it is the process by which prospective adoptive parents identify what they truly have the capacity for. Not every person/couple may be prepared to bring their best self to every situation; that is ok. This is a time to identify one's limits without fear of judgment. When my husband and I were adopting, another adoptive parent gave us this advice, "It's ok to say no to certain situations." It was, perhaps, the single most important piece of advice we received. Knowing your capacity and articulating your limits is an important beginning to creating an emotionally healthy family.

**A Few More Words About Race**

According to the Office of the Assistant Secretary for Planning and Evaluation (ASPE) of the Department of Health & Human Services, approximately one-quarter of all adoptions are transracial adoptions.

(https://aspe.hhs.gov/sites/default/files/private/pdf/264526/MEPA-Graphical-Factsheet.pdf).

If you're wondering what the heck "transracial adoption" is, don't worry; it was a new term for us, too. Transracial Adoption refers to the experience of adopting a child who is of a race outside of your own. It's a pretty simple concept with a complex name. That's because there is, indeed, a great deal of complexity associated with being a race that is different than your child's.

Many, including some adoption agencies, romanticize transracial adoption, indicating that parents can be "colorblind" when raising their children or proclaim that "love is enough." Let me dispel those notions right now—you cannot be colorblind, and love is not enough. In fact, you must see color, and you must indeed love, but you must also do more than that ... for the sake of your children. We must recognize that "...transracial adoptees cope with the double trauma of adoption and racism ..." (NPR-Illinois, Jan. 24, 2023, "The journey of transracial adoption") and be prepared to take the necessary action to effectively support our children. In a TIME article entitled "The Realities of Raising a Kid of a Different Race," author Karen Valby asserts, "Part of loving your child is seeing and loving the color of her skin—and accepting the reality that she will likely be painfully pigeonholed sometime in her life because of it"

(https://time.com/the-realities-of-raising-a-kid-of-a-different-race/).

As part of a child's health development, parents who are a race other than their children have a responsibility to help their children stay connected to their racial identity. This will mean helping to build a community of other people who look like them, becoming familiar with the experiences of others who share the same race as your child, educating yourself on any history of oppression experienced by that race, and, perhaps, most importantly, being aware of your own biases and being willing to "unlearn" all you may have been explicitly or implicitly taught about that race.

**Post-Adoption**

We were very fortunate to have held both our girls within hours after their birth, and both left the hospital in our arms. There was much that led up to that moment, but in the instant our feet hit the sidewalk, just beyond the sliding glass doors of the hospital, our world was forever changed. We were parents, just like that! Not only did we have new identities that we needed to acclimate to, but we were also responsible for helping to shape the development of these two precious darlings, providing them with the hope, confidence, strength, humility, love, and courage to propel them in life while helping them to understand their adoption, connect with their racial identify and promote a positive relationship with their biological families. Their time on this Earth could still be counted in hours, yet our journey as a family was already well on its way.

Every family's journey is special and unique, and we can all benefit from shared storytelling. In the interest of that collective learning, I offer some things our family does that we hope will help our children grow strong, confident, and proud of who they are and the families that love them.

Adoption Books – We created unique adoption books for each of our girls. These books tell the stories of how their adoption came to be and include pictures of their biological families and other people who were important to the adoption process.

"Adoptiversary" – every year, we celebrate the day their adoptions were finalized in court. We call it "Adoptiversary Day." We honor this family holiday by taking the day off from school or work and doing some kind of special family activity.

Open Dialogue with Biological Family – Both our girls have different degrees of openness with their biological families. For our youngest, we share letters and pictures with her biological mom. The relationship with our oldest daughter's biological family is much more open—we are friends on social media, we email, and we attend (in person) important life events.

Transparency – we have never hidden from our girls that they were adopted (as two men whose race is different than their daughters', it would be pretty hard to hide this). We allow our daughters to ask anything and answer those questions honestly in age-appropriate ways.

Racial Identity – we are fortunate to live in a "minority-majority community," so our girls mostly see other people who look like them. We are intentional about friend groups. We've had to learn how to "do hair" and visit the ethnicity-specific salons. We do not shy away from conversations about color and have open and age-appropriate) discussions about the different ways people have been and are treated based on the color of their skin. We participate in social cause activities with our girls and explain the meaning behind these events.

Like all parents, we are far from perfect. We often fail and sometimes epically fail. When we do, we role model taking accountability and practicing grace and forgiveness. And, like all other parents, we hope we've done enough (we probably haven't) and don't become the subject of our kids' future conversations with their therapists (we probably will).

This chapter opened with the goal that you may gain a bit more appreciation for the unique complexities of being the parent of adopted children. I hope I've given you a glimmer into some of that. Being a parent is hard. It is no more or less hard to be an adoptive parent—being an adoptive parent just has different layers.

Finally, to continue learning from others' experiences, I invite you to share your experiences with me. Perhaps, if enough of you do, I will create a specific website just for us or start a blog so we can all be in this space together.

## About the Author

Tom Tracy is the award-winning author of books in the *Scoochie & Skiddles Inclusive Kids Books Collection*. He has been featured on *CBS-Philly, South Jersey Magazine, and Gay Parent Magazine* and is a frequent guest on national podcasts. Tom is committed to helping fill a significant representation gap of diverse families in kids' books. Tom draws inspiration from his experience as an adoptive parent, a former foster parent, and from the countless families and children with whom he has had the privilege to serve as a licensed clinical social worker. Tom, his husband, and their two daughters live in the NJ suburbs of Philadelphia.

tomtracybooks.com

omtracybooks@gmail.com

# Chapter 24

# Parenting a Parent: Entering Their Reality

Alfredo Botello

I felt blindsided. I didn't know what was happening. My mom, the hero of my life, a single mom who, after her divorce in the 1970s, picked herself up and took belly dancing lessons, joined Toastmasters to become a better public speaker, joined the Sierra Club to take hikes and meet new friends, perhaps a new romantic partner, who quit smoking, who put me through private high school, who, when I was nineteen, asked me to teach her how to drive the freeway (she had only ever driven surface streets and was terrified of the freeway), was now saying to me, over and over, a constant refrain, "I just can't get it together."

This was six years ago. She was seventy-nine. She would stare at the paper calendar on the fridge, trying to write down an upcoming appointment with a doctor, or maybe the person who cut her hair, in the right box. But she couldn't. That calendar was covered in cross-outs. She'd ask me what her own scrawl meant. She would ask me, thirty seconds after taking her heart medication, whether she had taken it yet.

I didn't understand what was happening. I resented it. If her refrain was "I just can't get it together," my refrain became "What's *wrong* with you?" And I didn't ask with a soft, compassionate heart. My tone was snippy and judgmental. What had happened to the independent woman I knew growing up? Why was she so needy, confused, and anxious all the time?

I got a call from a greeter at Wal-Mart, nervously asking me to come to the parking lot, where my mom was in tears and in a panic because she couldn't find her car, which, when I arrived, was fifty feet away. I snapped at her, "How did you not see it? Making me come here. This is ridiculous." I felt pressured to be by her side all the time. I was already answering emails for her and handling bills. I thought these were all just "senior moments," and I quietly berated myself for being an impatient, selfish, ungrateful son.

And then we finally got the news. It was at a geriatric doctor's appointment: mom likely had onset Alzheimer's. For a moment, I was comforted: here was a diagnosis that explained the changes in mom. In the next moment, though, I felt ashamed. I had been unkind to someone I loved who could not help and did not understand what was happening to her mind.

The next six years were some of the most challenging of my life as I became her primary caretaker, the organizer of her life. The learning curve was steep. Being flexible and open to improvisation was the order of the day (and I'm a Virgo, so this was no small ask!) I made and revised "daily med checklist" sheets until they were simple enough for Mom to check off and understand. I became her power of attorney to help with finances and to make sure she would not fall prey to scammers. I paid her bills. She desperately wanted to continue living alone in her condo—that independent streak I knew as a child still shone through. I tried to help arrange Lyft, Uber, Instacart, and free shuttle buses to help her. This was after the DMV revoked her license because of the official diagnosis of dementia. And all the workarounds and improvisations worked—until they didn't. Whenever I thought we had found a "solution" to a problem, Mom's condition seemed to worsen. I had to find something else: I moved Mom closer to me and found an assisted living home (she refused to call it a home for the first three or four months, instead calling it "the hotel").

At first, I fought and argued, correcting her that I was not her brother Joe, who had died twenty-six years before. Explaining to her that no, she was wrong; the caretakers at "the hotel," in all likelihood, hadn't stolen her reading glasses. We'd argue. She'd cry. I felt awful. But I was technically "right," didn't that matter?

No. It didn't.

Over time, I realized something. The most compassionate thing I could do for both of us was to enter her reality. I can't point to one moment and say I had an epiphany or anything like that. It was more that I was exhausted by my resentment and frustration. I had to let my angry outer shell crack and break. When we went to Starbucks, I would see her fussing over any baby, toddler, or puppy we saw. So, at first, to pass the time as she drank her decaf latte, I would look up YouTube videos of puppies and kittens—ideally puppies *and* kittens playing *with* babies—and show them to her on my laptop. She smiled and laughed. My stomach began to unclench. I smiled, too. When we went to the supermarket, and she wanted chocolate, I'd buy her the family-size bag of Hershey's Kisses, and I saw her share some with the other residents at "the hotel." Only now, she wasn't calling it the hotel. She was calling it "the home." She would gossip about how this or that person working at the front desk was her favorite or least favorite. She would tell me she won fifty cents at bingo or maybe lost twenty-five cents. But I could hear her voice's joy and mental engagement when she shared these little moments. I could see she was happier. When she wanted to send a greeting card to an old friend but couldn't remember where she put her address book, I assured her, "Don't worry, I'll take care of it, Mom." I had put all her friends' addresses in my phone.

And I noticed something. About myself. I felt closer to my mom. I was entering her reality. It's not that I was actively trying to imagine what it must be like to have dementia; it's that I stopped fighting and stopped trying to make her be the mom she was when I was a boy. If she asked when her brother Joe was coming over, I told her, "I'll double-check." When she accused a caretaker of stealing her reading glasses, I would say, "Don't worry, I'll follow up on that." Then I might show her another cute video, comment on the weather, or offer her some special candy (she is partial to those little chocolate balls wrapped in gold foil). She became distracted and forgot about what had been causing her anxiety and agitation. Change was the constant; if I could bend with it and not break, we'd both be much happier.

When my older son was in high school, he loved football: he played it, watched his beloved Oakland Raiders on television, hated their rivals, the San Francisco 49ers and Denver Broncos, and talked player stats all day long. I had never been a sports guy, but I wanted to connect with my son. Soon, I became an Oakland Raiders fan. I attended all my son's high school games, working the snack shack or "chain gang." I took him to a few Raiders games. *I entered his reality.* It brought us closer. Was this so different from nodding along when my mom told me for the fourth or fifth time about a movie she watched and enjoyed? Or buying her replacement reading glasses, which she thought a caretaker had stolen, and telling her, "I put them in the wrong place, Mom. But look, I found them." She feels my sympathy, even if she no longer understands my every word, and we connect.

Words. Language. Reason. If mom can't think of the right word or follow a complex thought, that's okay because I know that holding her hand is much more eloquent and meaningful for both of us than words. When she reminds me for the eighth time not to forget that she wants cotton rounds and moisturizer from the drugstore, I don't snap at her anymore. I don't say, "I didn't forget. You already told me!" I just say, "We'll get it after coffee." I know we'll go to the drugstore one way or the other, so why not try to do it without the resentment? Why not try to do it with patience and good humor? I don't always succeed, but my heart and gut know the difference. My body tells me in no uncertain terms that patience and compassion benefit *both of us*.

The other day, she asked me to take her to church to hear the music. She comes from a Catholic family but, like me, isn't very religious. But she loves traditional songs and monks chanting. She prefers the old Latin Mass to its current vernacular form. It reminds her of growing up in an Austrian refugee camp after World War II. I knew the local church wouldn't have the "religious music" she had in mind, and six years ago, I would've argued with her and told her we were not going because it wouldn't be the music she wanted. She would have protested, but I would have held firm, and we wouldn't have gone. But the shell had broken. That Sunday, I took her anyway. We arrived mid-Mass (I didn't want to sit through an entire mass to hear whatever music might be played–that was my gift to myself), and within ten minutes, the choir played music and sang. It was an acoustic guitar, not chanting by monks. It wasn't what my mom expected. After the song ended, she nodded, saying we could leave. Back outside, in front of the church, she turned to me and said, "That was beautiful. Thank you."

I wish I had been more patient and compassionate from the beginning. But this has been my journey, too, and there have been a lot of detours and stumbling blocks along the way. And there will undoubtedly be more. I'm learning to forgive myself for those stumbles. I'm learning to accept that no one is perfect (not even a perfectionist Virgo!). I'm learning that what I can give to Mom in the way of patience, affection, and kindness gets repaid to me tenfold. That Sunday was perfect for me, too. My mom—my hero—was happy. My heart was full.

If you have a loved one with dementia, try to remember that their reality has changed. If you can, enter that reality. Embrace it if you can. Shrug and tolerate it if you can't. Is it exhausting and frustrating to be a caretaker? Yes, it is. Did you sign up for this? No. But can it also bring you closer to your loved one in ways you never imagined? Can it help you develop a capacity for compassion and patience you never knew you had? Yes. It can. If you're like me, it'll take time, and it might not be easy. There will be plenty of setbacks along the way, but I'm happy to report it's worth the effort.

For both of you.

## About the Author

Alfredo Botello is a novelist and screenwriter who has worked on projects ranging from the indie Sundance Global Short *La Revolucion De Iguodala* to the studio tent pole *Fast and Furious 9*. His debut novel, *180 Days*, has garnered multiple literary awards. He is a Fulbright Fellow in architecture and a Nicholl Fellow in screenwriting. In addition to screenplays and the novel, he has written for *The San Francisco Examiner Magazine, Metropolis, Diablo, Surface, The Utne Reader, Style, The East Bay Express,* and *The Monthly.* His next novel, *Spin Cycle,* about the challenges of caring for an aging parent with dementia, will be published by Koehler Books on January 14, 2025.

alfredobotello.com

alfredobotello@aol.com

# Chapter 25

## Speak Up and Stay Alive

Patricia J. Rullo

A doctor gently grasped my arm in the hospital hallway. I did not know him, and his visit was unannounced. In a hushed voice, he asked me to join him in a small room just outside the cardiac intensive care unit where my mom was fighting for her life. As the door closed behind us, another door opened, leading me into a world of fear, anger, disbelief, and—ultimately—strength. He had learned through the hospital network system that she had suffered a severe myocardial infarction after shoulder surgery. Two days after her heart attack, he took it upon himself to find me to share information that he asked me to keep confidential. He handed me a yellow envelope and said, "This stinks, and you need to do something about it."

Ten days earlier, Mom, who was seventy-eight years old, fell while working at a bridal shop. While retrieving a veil for a customer, she tripped over a two-inch-high threshold between the stock room and the showroom. She fell forward, absorbing the full impact with her shoulder. The city had cited the faulty threshold as a building violation long before the shop opened for business. It was one of many violations the shop owner felt free to ignore. The city also chose to overlook the violations and permitted the shop to open to the public with unchecked and unresolved safety hazards. Because the accident happened at work, the incident was reported to the Bureau of Workers' Compensation. To add insult to the injury, the shop owner had not paid the premiums in over a year. With no coverage in place, the owner was liable for all medical bills. A little string pulling, some political mumbo-jumbo, and a check for eight hundred dollars put the shop owner in the clear. It makes me wonder why employers bother paying Workers' Compensation premiums. However, that is another story for another time.

The fall crushed Mom's right shoulder. Repairing it called for surgery. The surgeon recommended a reverse total shoulder replacement, a unique procedure that switches the ball and socket. It is a highly technical surgery in which a metal ball is attached to the shoulder bone, and a plastic socket is connected to the upper arm bone.

Mom was scheduled for surgery on the following Monday. After we arrived at the hospital, the staff prepared her for surgery. We waited for four hours until they sent us home because the surgeon "didn't feel well." Interestingly enough, as we headed out of the hospital, I saw the surgeon exiting the elevator, drinking coffee, and laughing with another doctor. They strolled out, talking and joking around. I am not a doctor, but he didn't look sick to me. After three days of stressful attempts to reach the surgeon and cryptic conversations with his not-so-helpful secretary, they rescheduled the surgery for Thursday. Mom was feeling ill the day before the surgery. We chalked it up to nerves, yet looking back, she may have been showing signs of a heart attack.

The morning of the procedure, during the pre-surgery assessment, Mom's blood pressure was 80/55. She complained of not feeling well. The assistant anesthesiologist (who, incidentally, had his license suspended a few weeks later for stealing anesthesia drug waste to support his own drug habit) looked at the head anesthesiologist with concern in his eyes and asked her, "What about the blood pressure reading?" She ignored him. The surgeon walked in and asked to view the pre-op test results from the X-rays and electrocardiogram (ECG) Mom had taken a few days earlier. They were nowhere to be found. Despite several phone call requests from the lab and me, his secretary failed to forward them. The surgeon laughed and blamed it on the lab, saying, "That's the Greenfield lab for you."

Despite Mom's warning signs, the shoulder surgery took place. I sat in the waiting room from 5:30 a.m. until 10:15 a.m., when the surgeon came out and said Mom was in recovery and I could see her in forty-five minutes. Eleven o'clock came and went. I watched the surgeon and his assistant leave the hospital and enter the parking garage. At noon, I questioned the woman at the reception desk, and she told me Mom was in "pain management." Finally, at 1:15, I was allowed to enter the recovery room. Mom's skin was pale gray. She complained repeatedly, "I don't feel good. I don't feel good." When asked where she felt pain, she pointed to her chest. With that, one of the nurses gave her an injection of Versed, a sedative that stopped Mom's words before she could complete the sentence. The last thing I heard her say was, "I don't feel..." and they sent me out of the room.

At 3:20, the receptionist called me back into the recovery room. Seconds later, the nurses ushered me out. At 4:30, a nurse came out to the waiting room with a panicked look. "Your mother is having a heart attack, and we have to get her to the operating room as soon as possible," she said. The staff scrambled once again to find the pre-op ECG results to use as a comparison; however, thanks to the indifferent surgeon and his secretary, the prior test results were not there.

If not for the mystery doctor, who risked his job and his reputation to share his findings with me, I would not have known what actually happened the morning of Mom's surgery. Based on the nonchalant attitude of the surgeon and anesthesiologist, I was suspicious of their desire to complete the surgery. Yet, nothing prepared me for what was inside the yellow envelope. As we sat at the small conference table, the mystery doctor showed me a copy of the ECG taken two days earlier, at 10:53 the morning of the surgery. It showed not only the squiggly lines on the rhythm strip, which, as a layperson, I did not understand, but written at the top of the page were the words, heart attack in progress. He then showed me the results from the follow-up ECGs taken around 1:00, 3:00, and again at 4:20. All showed clear signs of heart trouble. At 10:53, a heart attack was in progress, which means she had likely been having heart trouble before that, perhaps even during surgery. At 11:00, the surgeon sauntered out of the building, either unaware of the heart attack or because his part of the job was over. In addition, an entire post-surgery staff and anesthesiologists had failed to recognize and follow up on what should have been evident to any medical professional.

In the days and weeks that followed, it became apparent the hospital was well aware of the potential for a wrongful death lawsuit if Mom were to die. They bent over backward to offer special treatments and proposed a surgery not ordinarily performed on a person of Mom's age. This 'salvage surgery,' as they called it, involved a seldom-used procedure using a right ventricular assist device performed by an outstanding surgeon. They gave Mom the only closed-door private room in the intensive care unit. Everyone was doing everything possible to keep her alive. I was in an interesting position in that I knew all the details of the undiagnosed heart attack, and yet no one knew that I knew. This allowed me to observe behavior, watch body language, and have pointed conversations with subsequent surgeons, doctors, and hospital staff. I took this time to gather information to complete the facts surrounding the grievous mistake.

So began four months of Mom's repeated brushes with death—all because of human error and carelessness on the part of the hospital and its staff.

I witnessed many adverse events during Mom's experience. She endured every hospital-acquired infection available. Several events resulted in formal hospital-documented incident reports. Certain staff members were prohibited from entering Mom's room. For example, I watched a surgeon attempt to insert drainage tubes to remove fluid that was accumulating in Mom's chest. In the process, he punctured one of her lungs, causing blood and fluid to spray around the room. Another doctor ushered me out, but I remained in the hallway, watching as at least a dozen nurses ran in and out of the room with blood transfusions and other lifesaving devices. To make matters worse, during these frantic moments, the power went out, sirens blared, and a lockdown was mandated through the public address system. The convergence of these events set the tone for the incomprehensible trials we faced almost daily.

A week later, a friendly but overly talkative nurse accidentally administered epinephrine (also known as adrenaline) instead of the intended drug, the antibiotic Vancomycin. The mistake was noticed by my daughter just before Mom went into cardiac arrest. Meanwhile, every few days, the shoulder surgery anesthesiologist, who was mainly responsible for the missed heart attack, and her assistant would surreptitiously peer into Mom's room while exchanging furtive and knowing glances with each other. They were not a part of Mom's care team and had no reason to hang around her room. They had no idea I knew about the life-threatening error or that I kept a watchful eye on their suspicious rounds.

The shoulder surgeon made it a point to be unavailable. Eighteen hours after Mom's shoulder surgery, she was back in the operating room for her second heart surgery. I ran into him in the hospital hallway. Nervously, he offered, "Oh, I just saw your Mom a few minutes ago. She looks good." I answered, "Really? Where did you see her? She's been in surgery for the last five hours." I was shocked that he so freely lied to me.

Throughout the rest of Mom's stay, his absence and elusiveness continued. Mom's doctors, surgeons, and nurses held a family meeting every Friday to inform me of her progress. Each week, I requested his attendance. Each week, he phoned in with an excuse. One evening, I saw him enter the ICU. I crossed his path and asked him directly what went on during the morning of Mom's shoulder surgery. He danced back and forth, slipped his shoe on and off, and said, "Had I known what I do today, I would have done things differently. The anesthesiologist didn't tell me your Mom was having a heart attack." His body language and ambiguous answers left me knowing there was more to the story. I never saw him again. He didn't return—not even to remove her stitches. Four months later, a nurse at the rehabilitation center noticed nylon threads hanging from Mom's shoulder. She removed them herself while shaking her head in disbelief. I found out a few years later—he had been promoted!

For weeks, Mom needed a ventilator to help her breathe. She was intubated with an endotracheal tube inserted through her mouth. The tube was tied with thin straps around her face and taped into place on her cheeks. Bound and gagged, she looked like a prisoner. The pressure from the straps caused serious skin breakdown to her lips. She was unable to speak or move and was groggy from drugs. In an effort to communicate, I recited each letter of the alphabet until she stopped me with a slight eyebrow movement that I often missed. Sometimes, this spelling exchange took hours and made it difficult for me to understand her concerns.

One morning, through this obscure method of dialogue, Mom indicated pain at her urine catheter site. All day, I begged the nurse to change it. She always had an excuse. At the end of the day, as I headed toward the exit door, I saw the nurse waiting in the hallway with the new catheter package. I turned around to see her enter Mom's room and headed back. I watched, and it became clear why she had not changed the catheter while I was there. She obviously did not know how to do it. She unfolded the directions accompanying the tubing kit and placed them on the bed. Then, she turned the tube in many directions, trying to match the pictures on the paper. When I noticed she was not wearing gloves, I entered the room and asked her to send a nurse qualified to change a urine catheter.

Early the next morning, I entered Mom's room to find her feet bound with bloody gauze. I unraveled the gauze and saw all ten of her toenails mangled and torn as if someone had used a machete to cut them. I flew out of the room to the nurse's station to demand an explanation. For some reason, a local podiatrist had made his rounds in the middle of the night to perform his ghoulish "pedicures." "Oh yeah," one of the nurses responded, "We get complaints about him all the time." I promised them that if Mom got an infection, I would take serious measures to address this heartless and macabre action.

Two weeks later, my mind was shattered once again as I watched a senior physician teach a roomful of interns how to clean a bedsore. As the students gathered at Mom's bedside, the doctor wandered across the room to the windowsill where I kept my Clorox wipes. (Each morning, I wiped every surface in the room in an attempt to keep the germs at bay.) Somehow, the doctor had spotted the wipes, and before anyone could react, he pulled several out of the container and proceeded to wipe the bedsore with Clorox bleach. The hospital filed another incident report, and the doctor was banned from Mom's room.

These are only a few bizarre and unimaginable events that occurred right before me. I wonder how many other mistakes happened when I was not there. However, despite the constant calamities—many highly competent doctors, nurses, and hospital staff eventually saved the day.

Throughout this experience, I felt fear, entered the unknown, and emerged as a wiser medical consumer with a message to share. When life presents challenging assignments, I always ask myself, "What am I supposed to do with this information?" The writing of the book *Speak Up and Stay Alive—the Patient Advocate Hospital Survival Guide* was my answer. If my mom's experience helps another person, there is a positive reason for her journey.

The point of my story? Learn how to be your own advocate. Try to have an advocate with you during a hospital stay.

I hope you feel empowered to speak up during every healthcare or hospital encounter. Remember, you have to Speak Up and Stay Alive.

**About the Author**

Patricia J. Rullo is the author of several healthcare books, including *Your Guide to Healthcare Acquired Infections, Healthcare and Hospital Hazards, Highway to Heart, Humor, and Honesty in Healthcare,* a patient safety/charity anthology, and *Speak Up and Stay Alive,* a hospital survival guide for patient advocates. She is a speaker and trainer on patient safety and also hosts and produces three syndicated radio shows - "Speak Up and Stay Alive," "Authors on Fire," and "Eleven Cats Radio."

Pat is a seasoned audiobook narrator and producer and offers her radio experience to help others host their own podcasts.

She founded the Firebird Book Awards and the Positive Change Podcast Awards. The submission fees are tax-deductible donations that contribute to Pat's mission to help transform homeless shelters for women and children by providing them with handmade pillowcases and children's bedtime books.

She recently launched Firebird Inked, a self-publishing service that covers everything from editing to cover design, formatting, and Amazon uploading while protecting the author's royalties.

Rescued by 13 cats, Pat is quite an accomplished litter box scooper.

speakuptalkradio.com

pr@speakuptalkradio.com

# Afterword

The stories we have explored together reflect the rich tapestry of human experience. They illuminate the cracks in our institutions, pointing us to opportunities for transformation. With their unique backgrounds and insights, the authors have bravely exposed their vulnerabilities and shared their strengths, reminding us that healing is as much about connection and empathy as it is about medical intervention.

In a world where the clinical often overshadows the compassionate, these narratives challenge the status quo. They invoke a call to action for all of us—healthcare providers, patients, families, and advocates—to engage more deeply in the conversations that shape our health outcomes. They underscore the necessity of listening not just to the language of medicine but to the voices of those who navigate illness, treatment, and care on a daily basis.

Moving forward, let us carry the lessons and reflections gleaned from this anthology into our interactions. Let us advocate for patient-centered approaches that honor the whole person, recognizing that health is not a destination but a journey to be traveled with intention and support.

*Wellness Through Words* is an invitation to examine our roles within the healthcare framework and commit to active participation in shaping a more compassionate landscape. May we all emerge from these pages inspired to share our stories, amplify the voices of others, and continuously seek pathways for healing and understanding.

As you close this book and reflect on its contents, may you carry forward not just the ideas presented here but also the spirit of collective healing that permeates these pages. Words have power—the power to heal, to challenge, and to connect. Let us wield that power with purpose, paving the way for a brighter, safer, and more empathetic future in healthcare.

Thank you for joining us on this journey. Together, let us amplify our voices and advocate for the wellness we truly deserve.

Made in United States
Orlando, FL
18 November 2024